BRIGHT NOTES

BILLY BUDD
BY
HERMAN MELVILLE

Intelligent Education

Nashville, Tennessee

BRIGHT NOTES: Billy Budd
www.BrightNotes.com

No part of this publication may be used or reproduced in any manner whatsoever without written permission, except in the case of brief quotations in critical articles and reviews. For permissions, contact Influence Publishers http://www.influencepublishers.com.

ISBN: 978-1-645422-06-8 (Paperback)
ISBN: 978-1-645422-07-5 (eBook)

Published in accordance with the U.S. Copyright Office Orphan Works and Mass Digitization report of the register of copyrights, June 2015.

Originally published by Monarch Press.
Edward R. Winans; James Paris, 1966
2020 Edition published by Influence Publishers.

Interior design by Lapiz Digital Services. Cover Design by Thinkpen Designs.

Printed in the United States of America.

Library of Congress Cataloging-in-Publication Data forthcoming.
Names: Intelligent Education
Title: BRIGHT NOTES: Billy Budd
Subject: STU004000 STUDY AIDS / Book Notes

CONTENTS

1) Introduction to Herman Melville — 1

2) Background on Billy Budd — 5

3) A Note on the Style of Billy Budd — 9

4) Textual Analysis
    - Preface, Chapters 1–9 — 14
    - Chapters 10–19 — 31
    - Chapters 20–27 — 54
    - Chapters 28–31 — 74

5) Character Analyses — 80

6) Critical Commentary — 84

7) Essay Questions and Answers — 89

8) Glossary of Nautical Terms — 95

9) Bibliography and Guide to Research — 98

HERMAN MELVILLE

INTRODUCTION

MELVILLE'S LIFE

(1819-1891) Born into a family of substantial means in New York City on August 19, 1819, Herman Melville spent a secure and comfortable childhood. His maternal grandfather, Peter Gansevoort, had served as a general in the American Revolution, and his father, Allan Melvill (his father's spelling for the family name) was a successful importer. In 1830, however, his father suffered heavy financial reverses which were followed by serious illness culminating in his death in 1832.

Shocked by the death of his father whom he idolized, Melville moved with his family to Albany where he attended the Albany Classical School for a time. Here, constant friction with his mother, and his own restlessness soon brought an end to his spotty education, supplemented only by his avid reading of the books from his father's library.

Melville soon drifted into a variety of occupations. He worked for a time as a clerk in a store owned by an older brother, as a messenger for a bank, and later, as a country schoolteacher near his uncle's home in Pittsfield, Massachusetts. Finally in 1839, he signed on a British merchant ship, the St. Lawrence, bound to Liverpool and back, a trip which provided the material for his novel, *Redburn* (1849), and the impetus for an extended period of travel and adventure. Although he again tried school teaching on his return from Liverpool, he signed aboard the whaler Acushnet as an ordinary seaman in 1841.

After a trip around Cape Horn, Melville suffered the hardship of life aboard a mid-nineteenth century whaler until he could no longer tolerate it. Accordingly, he and a shipmate Tobias Greene (who appears as Toby in *Typee*) deserted the St. Lawrence at Nukuheva in the Marquesas Islands. Here Melville spent a month as the captive of a cannibal tribe, and finally escaped aboard the Australian whaler the Lucy Ann, which he left a short time later at Tahiti. Again after a short stay working at a variety of occupations, he signed aboard the whaler Charles and Henry, and arrived in Hawaii in April, 1843. Here, after working for a short time as a warehouse clerk, by now homesick for America, he joined the U.S. Navy and was assigned to the frigate United States. Fourteen months later, after visits to Mexico and South America, he was finally discharged in New York City in October, 1844, and with the exception of a few trips later in his life, he closed forever the period of his adventures.

In the years immediately following his travels, Melville began his career as a writer. In 1846 he published *Typee*, a somewhat exaggerated and imaginative account of his stay among the Typee islanders, and in 1847, its sequel *Omoo*. These were followed by *Mardi*, in 1849, an allegorical novel quite different from its predecessors and the precursor of *Moby Dick*. Attempting to atone for the failure of *Mardi*, Melville returned to the method of his earlier adventure books with *Redburn* (1849), which borrowed material from his first voyage to Liverpool in 1839; and *White Jacket* (1850), which enlarged upon his experience as a seaman aboard the United States.

Although his first five books had won him considerable fame and some small measure of financial security, Melville still felt dissatisfied with his work, and in 1851 he published *Moby Dick*, which although a failure in its day, has proved in the twentieth century to be his most famous work.

It was also during these first few years at home following his travels that Melville became established as an important member of the New York literary group, and became a friend of Nathaniel Hawthorne, whose encouragement was of immeasurable aid in the writing of *Moby Dick*. So much so in fact that Melville dedicated the book to him with the following inscription: "In token of my admiration for his genius this book is inscribed to Nathaniel Hawthorne."

In 1847, Melville married Elizabeth Shaw, the daughter of the Chief Justice of Massachusetts, and had in the fall of that year moved from Pittsfield, Massachusetts to New York City. Later, early in 1850, after a brief trip to London to make arrangements for the publication of *White Jacket*, he moved to "Arrowhead," a farm in Pittsfield, Massachusetts where he was to remain for the next thirteen years.

Unfortunately for Melville the critical reaction to *Moby Dick* was negative, and the reaction to *Pierre* (1852), a somewhat confused and melodramatic novel which attacked, among other things, conventional morality and publishing practices, was even worse. Disturbed by his waning popularity and in ill health, Melville turned for a time to writing articles and short stories for the magazines Putnam's and Harper's. Among his works in this period are *Israel Potter* (1855), which had been first published serially, and *Piazza Tales* (1856), a collection of short stories which included the now famous "Bartelby, the Scrivener" and "Benito Cereno." In 1857, he published the last novel in his lifetime, *The Confidence Man*, a satiric tale which has its setting on a Mississippi River steamboat, and which like *Moby Dick* has aroused much recent critical interest.

His career now at its lowest ebb, ill and in debt, Melville traveled through the Mediterranean countries and the Holy Land on borrowed money, and on his return attempted to make his living lecturing on such subjects as "statuary in Rome" and "the South Seas." Unsuccessful, he sold his farm at Pittsfield, paid his debts with the remaining money, and bought a house in New York City where he secured a job in the Custom House which he held until his retirement in 1885.

During these years and those which followed, Melville published several volumes of poetry, including: *Battle Pieces and Aspects of the War* (1866), *Clarel: a Poem and a Pilgrimage in the Holy Land* (1876), *John Marr and Other Sailors* (1888), and *Timoleon* (1891). These last three volumes were for the most part privately printed in small editions at the expense of an uncle, Peter Gansevoort.

At his death on September 28, 1891, Melville left in manuscript a considerable number of verses as well as the short novel, *Billy Budd*, which was not published until 1924. It has since proved one of his most interesting works, for in addition to accelerating an already reviving interest in Melville, it has achieved much critical acclaim.

BILLY BUDD

BACKGROUND

Written during the last years of Melville's life, *Billy Budd* in some respects represents a resolving of some of the problems which had beset Melville during his life. Always concerned with the place and welfare of man in a universe naturally hostile, and made even more so by the rising industrial revolution (which led to the economic upheavals of 1873-1879), Melville explores in *Billy Budd* the tragedy of man's inability to cope with the difficulties of his own creation. In those late years of his life following the Civil War, Melville lived through the chaos of reconstruction; the numerous government scandals; "Black Friday" 1870; the Tweed Ring in New York, 1871; the Haymarket Riots in Chicago, 1866; the growth of monopolies; the expansion of the west, and numerous other momentous movements and events. Gone now is the rebelliousness of the Captain Ahab of *Moby Dick*, and in its place there appears a spirit of quiet acceptance of the laws of society which condemn the guiltiness Billy, who, like so many, suffers injustice because of an inflexible social order.

And perhaps like Billy Budd, Melville came quietly to his own end. Always a religious skeptic, he was able, as his friend Hawthorne remarked of him, to "neither believe nor be comfortable in his disbelief, and he is too honest and courageous not to try to do one or the other." Rejecting early the stern Calvinism of his mother, he found life a series of paradoxes in which the good was inextricably interwoven with the evil.

Finally, *Billy Budd*, like most of Melville's work is at least partly autobiographic. Not only is the volume inscribed to Jack Chase, who had been a fellow foretopman with Melville many years before aboard the United States, but the story opens in Liverpool, the city to which he had traveled on his own first voyage, and it is from his own knowledge of the sea that he achieves **realism** in a novel otherwise filled with dark forebodings and veiled meanings.

The difficulties of Melville's career as a writer, of course, stemmed from many causes. First of all, his great books, *Moby Dick*, *The Confidence Man*, and *Billy Budd* could not achieve a great audience in their own time. They required, with their wealth of **allusion** and **imagery**, too much of the often simple and provincial American. Nor was it possible for his age to lightly accept the manifold criticisms which he leveled at society and its institutions, for Melville possessed none of the humorous talent of a Mark Twain who could make such criticisms palatable, nor could he emulate those writers of sentimental fiction whose simple and unsophisticated work passed for great literature. And lastly, Melville in his own way, as he had nearly always, wrote the books he wanted to write. As he said in *Pierre*, "I write precisely as I please."

BRIEF SUMMARY

In the year 1797, following the great mutinies in the British Navy at Spithead and Nore and during the first of the Napoleonic

Wars, the British Merchant ship Rights of Man is halted at sea by H. M. S. Indomitable. The Indomitable, in need of seamen, impresses the young foretopman of the Rights of Man, Billy Budd, into the King's service. Although Billy is a young man without either family or education, Lieutenant Ratcliffe, the impressment officer from the Indomitable, instantly recognizes him as a superior man. And though Billy does not make the same excellent impression among the more experienced sailors of the Indomitable, he is, nevertheless, noticed as a capable sailor by the officers of that vessel.

Captain "Starry" Vere of the Indomitable is a well-read, quiet and capable commander, respected by his officers and highly regarded by his superiors. The officers of his crew, though generally young, are capable and efficient, and the crewmen, though some have been involved in the recent mutinies, are in general experienced and loyal.

Among the petty officers of the Indomitable's crew is John Claggart, Master-at-arms, whose principal duty is to oversee the men of the main decks. He is a comparative newcomer to the Navy and has risen rapidly through the ranks to his present position of authority, the duties of which he performs by harassing all those who are under him. Although he appears perfectly sane, he is a man whose essential nature is unbalanced, a man whose violent nature is carefully concealed beneath a placid surface.

From their very first meeting Claggart nurses a hatred for Billy, "the Handsome Sailor," who appears the incarnation of all that is good in contrast to his own evil nature. Throughout their many meetings the good and simple Billy cannot grasp the fact that Claggart hates him and is plotting mischief for him. And even though he is warned by Dansker, an old sailor who befriends him, Billy cannot believe that anyone hates him.

Finally, Claggart unmasks his evil nature by accusing Billy of plotting mutiny among members of the crew. After amassing false evidence with the help of Squeak, one of the corporals of the gun deck who is his willing and unscrupulous tool, Claggart confronts Billy before Captain Vere with his accusations. Here Billy, shocked and unable to speak because of a speech impediment which affects him in moments of crisis, strikes out and accidentally kills Claggart.

Although Captain Vere is aware that Billy's action was both automatic and in some measure justified, he convinces the Court Marshal aboard ship, which he has hurriedly called because of the recent mutinies, of the need to maintain discipline. Accordingly, Billy is convicted and the next morning hanged from the yardarm, dying with the words "God bless Captain Vere" on his lips.

Later official accounts of the affair falsely record that Billy was an irresponsible killer, and Claggart a patriotic sailor killed in the performance of his duty. The truth, however, is somehow recorded among the simple men of the service who keep track of the spar from which Billy was hung and by one who writes a **ballad** telling the sad story of the good Billy's fate.

BILLY BUDD

A NOTE ON THE STYLE OF BILLY BUDD

....

Billy Budd, like many sea stories, was based on an actual event. Long engrossed by the famous Somers' Affair which had taken place years before when Melville was himself in the South Seas, he, late in his life, decided to reproduce the story of that event in narrative form. Melville, then, first wrote the story as a short tale under the title "Baby Budd, Sailor," which he later revised and expanded to more than twice its original length. Although an examination of the earlier draft reveals more action and fewer digressions, it was neither as effective nor as powerful as the final version in spite of its numerous digressions, allusions, and symbols.

Through the judicious use of his own knowledge of the sea, and a faithful, if somewhat imaginative, handling of the events of the Somers' Affair, Melville achieved in *Billy Budd* a novel that is both believable and realistic. Thus, recalling his own horror of flogging, and his own careful efforts to avoid even a reprimand, Melville created Billy much in his own image. Further, Melville borrowed from his past work as well as his past life. In *Billy Budd* a vicious and destructive Master-at-Arms is protected by the rank, as was Bland in *White Jacket*, and the Articles of War which harshly and irrevocably ruled the lives of seamen aboard men-of-war are again explored and excoriated. To these primary and personal sources, Melville added *The Naval History of Great Britain* by William James, the *Life of Nelson* by Robert Southy, and the *Mutiny at Nore*, a drama by Douglas Jerrold.

In *Billy Budd*, Melville also returned to a method of composition which he had used as a young man. First, he opened the novel by telling the story sketchily and providing necessary background, and then, he later expanded and broadened the tale by adding significant digressions which both heighten its effectiveness and intensify its meaning. Thus, the tale of Billy and his unhappy end assumes the quality of myth. Billy is at once both a man and an archetype, for not only is he a man but also the Adam of "Genesis" and of Milton's *Paradise Lost*.

Billy Budd as a novel, however, lacks the essential straightforward simplicity of the Biblical tale of man's fall because it is filled with what Melville himself termed ambiguities, and as a result admits of no clear-cut dogmatic interpretation. This concept of intentional ambiguity is perhaps best revealed by a sentence which Melville deleted from the final manuscript: "Here ends a story not unwarranted by what sometimes happens in this incomprehensible world of ours-innocence and infamy, spiritual depravity and fair repute." Thus, Melville's world, like his theology, is filled with uncertainties which he makes no claim to comprehend.

Not all of Melville's ambiguities, however, are the result of his allusiveness or of his inversions of narrative. In addition he employed innumerable stylistic devices to enrich the texture of his prose and to make it more meaningful. First among them, of course, is his use of symbol. For example, as Billy dies, the birds symbolically circle the ship like angels, and Billy's white clothes are a symbol of his innocence; the Indomitable symbolically triumphs over the Atheiste as Captain Vere ponders the question of truth; and at many points in the story Billy is variously Alexander the Great, Apollo, and Achilles; Claggart is Judas, Ananias, the serpent; Dansker, Merlin and Chiron. Thus each character becomes more than a man; they become, hero, philosopher, betrayer, and seer.

A further enrichment is gained by a consistent use of figurative speech, principally of **metaphor** and **simile**. Captain Vere is "like Montaigne"; Claggart is "as beardless as Tecumseh"; and Billy, when accused by Claggart, "looked struck as by white leprosy"; and following Billy's death the sky "was shot through with a soft glory as the fleece of the Lamb of God, ... and the sea "like smooth white marble.

To these more obvious techniques Melville added some that are more subtle. For example, although the story is told entirely in the past tense, the direct narrative portions (speech) are told in the present, and the actions of characters described through the use of the present participle to give a sense of immediacy. In addition the sound of the sentences, their very rhythms, are often portents of the action to come. Sentences are often long and somber with Miltonic phrasing and language. In the expository opening to Chapter Twenty-six, as Billy awaits execution, Melville relates that "the night so luminous on the spar deck but otherwise on the cavernous ones below, levels so like the tiered galleries of a coal mine - the luminous night passed away. But, like the prophet in the chariot disappearing in the heavens and dropping his mantle to Elisha, the withdrawing night transferred its pale role to the breaking day." Thus, the reader is prepared for the somber and sad events which the chapter is to relate. Or, for example, the heading to Chapter Thirteen, "Pale ire, envy and despair," a direct borrowing from Milton's *Paradise Lost* which both serves to introduce the chapter in which Claggart's personality is to be further explored, and by means of which, the **allusion** to the serpent-satan image is carefully reinforced.

Further and even more subtle methods by which Melville used style to either emphasize the nature of a character or to produce a particular mood are his use of inverted or unusual word orders and his symbolic use of color. For instance, Captain Vere's reflective qualities are foreshadowed when Melville describes him as an officer "unlike no few." Notice here that Melville avoids a direct description like not many of the king's officers, but uses instead an oblique and somewhat ambiguous manner in which to introduce him. The descriptions of Billy on the other hand always portray him in direct motion, climbing, talking, asking; and Claggart in indirect motion, waiting, watching, scheming. Then too, Billy's complexion is rose-red, while Claggart's is pale; Billy's hair is blond and Claggart's black; Billy's domain is the high mast against the blue sky; Claggart's the gloom of the lower gundeck.

Another interesting device by which Melville achieves part of the purpose of impressing upon the reader an unutterable sense of impending doom and the inevitability of events is his use of involuntary action and reaction on the part of various characters in the story. Captain Vere acts only in accordance with the Articles of War, often contrary to his personal beliefs; Billy involuntarily strikes and kills Claggart; Dansker is unable to warn Billy directly; Captain Vere utters "struck dead by an Angel of God," and even the crew responds involuntarily to Billy's final "God bless Captain Vere."

Thus, in *Billy Budd* Herman Melville, through the use of a seemingly endless variety of literary devices and allusions, unified and gave order and meaning to innumerable disconnected parts. In what is essentially a novelette, he achieved a profoundness which makes the reader return again and again to the story, each time to discover a new facet, a new idea, a new insight. And more, the novel's tight suspenseful narration, it symbolic allusions, Biblical, historical, and literary, and its haunting power upon the reader's mind cause him to ponder its weighty and profound philosophic and moral implications, and make it the great masterpiece of Melville's final years.

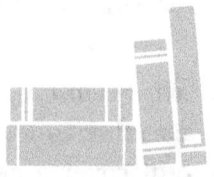

BILLY BUDD

TEXTUAL ANALYSIS

PREFACE, CHAPTERS 1-9

PREFACE

The year 1797 was a violent one. In 1775, the American Colonists had revolted; in 1789, the French had overthrown the monarchy; and now the French and English, hereditary enemies, were engaged in the first of the Napoleonic wars. Made bold, perhaps by the revolutionary spirit of the age, the sailors of the British fleet at Spithead and Nore had recently mutinied, seeking redress for some of the abuse and ill treatment then common. Although the mutinies were ended by the hanging of the ringleaders, some badly needed reforms were initiated as a result of them.

Comment

As in *Moby Dick* and most of his early adventure novels, Melville calls upon his knowledge of the sea to provide a background for his story. *Billy Budd*, published in 1924, thirty-three years after Melville's death, and sixty-seven years after the publication of his last novel, *The Confidence Man*, represents a return to the mode of *Moby Dick*, and a revival of his power as a writer of prose.

Historically, novelists who, like Melville, are interested in the eternal conflicts between good and evil, and problems of man's place in a seemingly hostile universe, have chosen a ship at sea for their setting. Here they may in the created microcosm, or miniature world, not only limit the action of their stories, but study the actions and reactions of a limited number of characters under carefully controlled conditions. Life aboard ship provides such a perfectly limited and miniature society, for here the relationships between human beings and the laws and regulations which govern those relationships are limited enough to allow an exploration deeper than would be possible if the action were to be set in a more complicated world.

And finally, the novel is set against a background of violence (the mutinies, the war with France) not merely to heighten the reader's interest, but so that the violence which occurs aboard the Indomitable may be weighed and contrasted with the greater violence which surrounds it. The deaths of two men are not less significant than the deaths of many, for in these carefully limited circumstances the reader is able to analyze and evaluate the causes and the results of violence; and even more important, to ponder the questions which Melville thus poses. Are law and justice one and the same thing? If man cannot achieve absolute justice in so limited a circumstance as posed in the novel, how can he hope to achieve it in the larger world?

Although Melville doesn't answer these questions, their implications are clear. If man is to outgrow violence and war, he must not allow himself to be ruled by inflexible and arbitrary codes as does Captain Vere by the Articles of War. If man is to succeed, he must be courageous enough to change those arbitrary codes and values by which he has allowed himself to be governed. Man must adopt more practical, and above all, more humane codes.

CHAPTER ONE

In the time before steamships, seamen on shore would often gather themselves about one of their number, who by his bearing and appearance was their superior. Such a one was Billy Budd, a foretopman in the British Navy. He had been but a short time since impressed on the high sea into the King's service from the merchantman Rights of Man, and was now serving aboard H.M.S. Indomitable. Lieutenant Ratcliffe of the Indomitable had selected Billy almost immediately after boarding the Rights of Man and Billy did not protest. Captain Graveling of the Rights of Man and Billy's shipmates were saddened to see him go, for Billy was Captain Graveling's "Jewel," the man who made for a happy ship, a "sweet and pleasant fellow" though a man to beware of in a fight. And so Billy had transferred his meager belongings in a sea bag to the Indomitable by way of that ship's cutter, and as they rowed toward the ship, he jestingly bade the Rights of Man "goodbye."

Though slightly annoyed by Billy's touching farewell, thinking it perhaps a slur at impressment in general and himself in particular, Lieutenant Ratcliffe put Billy's action down to high spirits. Surely Billy meant no slur, since he was basically a good hearted and simple man who accepted his impressment as another turn in his adventurous life.

Aboard the Indomitable Billy was soon assigned as foretopman, a duty which he found to his liking, an attitude unlike that of some of the other impressed men aboard who undoubtedly had families at home.

| Comment |

Very quickly in this short chapter, Melville has succeeded in introducing his major character and supplying most of the necessary background. The names of the ships involved are of course important to the **theme** of the novel. The Rights of Man (also the title of a famous work by Thomas Paine) and the natural and humane world which it represents is contrasted with the unnatural and inflexibly ordered world of the Indomitable. So too, is the name Billy Budd, which introduces a young man in the bloom of life. Like Billy, Melville himself had served as a foretopman during his early seafaring career aboard the warship United States. And significantly, the story opens at the docks of Liverpool where Melville had landed during his first sea voyage.

Numerous references, Biblical, historical, literary and mythical, serve to reinforce the noble nature of Billy's character and provide depth for the seemingly simple tale. Aloft, straddling the yard-arm, Billy is compared to Alexander the Great taming his warhorse, Bucephalus; or as a "superb figure" astride Taurus the bull, whose starry constellation is visible in the night sky, and finally to Apollo, the sun god. The Negro sailor who appears briefly in the opening paragraphs is portrayed as a descendant of Ham, youngest son of Noah whose descendants bear the curse of servitude. Among the varied historical references is that to Joachim Murat (1767? - 1815), the Dandy King of Naples who was an ally of Napoleon.

The Indomitable was a warship of seventy-four guns which made it fairly large. In those days ships were not rated as they are now, corvette, destroyer, cruiser, or battleship, though the name corvette still signifies a small warship; but rather by the number of guns which they could mount and the size of those guns. All naval sailing vessels then carried anywhere from two to four masts, each of which supported numerous sails.

CHAPTER TWO

Although Billy was received well by the crewmen of the Indomitable, he was not now the center of attention. Here, among the larger and more experienced crew of the warship, his youthful appearance set him even more apart than it had aboard the Rights of Man. He was regarded in general with quiet amusement by the battle hardened crewmen, and generally favorably by the officers.

Questioned by one of the officers as to his background, Billy revealed that he was a foundling. However, his appearance strongly suggested that he was of noble descent. Although he was illiterate, he was intelligent; although he could not read music, he could sing and often composed his own songs. Indeed, he seemed a perfect specimen of young manhood whose only imperfection was a tendency to stutter when under the stress of strong emotion.

Comment

Billy's character and appearance are here explored in considerable depth. He is compared to the Hercules of Greek mythology, a handsome and shapely figure; and to Adam, the simple man of paradise without vice. Billy's noble and simple nature is further underscored by a comparison of sailors in general with landsmen. Sailors not only lead simpler and less complicated lives, but when they do indulge in evil or violent activities (usually ashore), it is because they have been long at sea and have stored up energy to expend.

So too is the more civilized world of the Indomitable contrasted with that of the Rights of Man where crewmen in general are younger and more inexperienced. Thus Melville achieves a series of contrasts within the world of seamen, and each contrast serves to intensify and deepen the moral and philosophic significance of the story. He borrows heavily from the Christian doctrine that men in general are in a fallen state (the result of Adam's sin), and from Rousseau's (a French philosopher) idea of the "noble savage" (who argued that it was civilization and the effects of civilization which have corrupted man; that man in his natural or simple state was free of sin). Thus, Billy is Adam before the serpent, unlike those fallen men whose lives are corrupted by life in the cities. He is further compared with the mysterious Caspar Hauser, (1812?–1833) a young man of unknown, but of reputedly noble origin who had been assassinated in Nuremburg in 1833.

Again, the story is given depth by historical, religious and literary **allusion**; and like the tragic heroes of the ancient Greek drama, Billy is endowed with a fatal flaw (his stuttering) which will bring about his downfall.

The literary device of **foreshadowing** is of course evident in the allusion to Casper Hauser, and to Billy's new Eden, the Indomitable, which like every Eden has its serpent.

CHAPTER THREE

When Billy had been impressed on the Indomitable, that ship was on its way to join the Mediterranean fleet. After the ship had joined the fleet, it was assigned various tasks, one of which was to conduct scouting missions.

It was now the summer of 1797, just a few months after the famous mutinies at Spithead and at Nore in April and May of that year. These mutinies had deeply shocked and frightened the English. Not only were the English engaged in a war with France, but it seemed to most Britons that the mutineers had caught the fever of revolt from the French. Even the patriotic songs then written which stressed the deep patriotism of British sailors to the Crown seemed ironic. Indeed, the mutinies were a blow to the national pride, and like the American Revolution a few years before, they became events which British historians and writers in later years chose to ignore, and which when they did write of them at all, they did so discreetly.

Finally after much talk, the mutinies were put down by force and the red flag of the mutineers lowered, a conclusion made possible only by the general loyalty of the British marines and the fact that the mutineers were not fully supported by British sailors. In any event, thousands who had participated in the mutinies were again on active service aboard various ships, and, indeed, some of these same men were destined to be among those who made possible Lord Nelson's victories at the Nile and Trafalgar, and in a sense heroically restored that glory to the British Navy which it had so recently lost.

Comment

G. P. R. James (1799-1860) was a popular British historical novelist. Lord Nelson was of course England's most famous naval hero whose victories over the French at the Nile and Trafalgar (where he died after giving the famous command

"England expects every man to do his duty.") have remained one of the bright pages of English naval history.

In this chapter Melville's seeming digression serves to create suspense and to intensify the background against which the action of the story is to take place. We are carefully reminded that British commanders are uncomfortably aware that many of their crewmen were involved in or at least sympathetic with the mutinies at Spithead and Nore, a fact which will account for Captain Vere's action later in the book when he quickly sentences Billy to death. Under normal circumstances, he might have waited for the ship to return to port before holding Billy's trial.

CHAPTER FOUR

This chapter like the preceding one represents what Melville calls a bypath.

Over the past centuries warfare has undergone a number of great changes. The first major change of course was brought about by the introduction of gunpowder from China, and although early guns and cannons were awkward, they soon succeeded in making armed and armored knights obsolete. Although the new weapons had brought about a decline of chivalry, a few great seamen had managed to keep alive the old traditions of gallantry.

It is of course also true that there are those who believe that individual acts of heroism and gallantry are merely foolish exhibitions which have no place in modern warfare. Indeed, there are even those who would argue that the preservation of Nelson's battleship Victory with the star painted on the quarterdeck where the great sailor fell is mere foolishness, since after all Nelson had exposed himself willfully and unnecessarily to death at Trafalgar and did not therefore die valiantly.

Though these are the arguments of some, too great a care for personal safety is not a virtue in a military man. For even now the name of Nelson stirs the blood of military men more greatly than the name Wellington, a fact attested to by none other than Alfred Lord Tennyson, who called Nelson, "the greatest sailor since the world began." (From the "Ode on the Death of Wellington," 1852.)

Before his last and greatest victory at Trafalgar, Nelson had written his last will and testament and then had bravely gone forth to meet his death! Surely it is an act such as this and not a sense of prudence, which has the power, like great poetry, to inspire others.

Comment

Melville, like the teller of sea stories of old, often interrupts his narrative to intersperse bits and pieces of information to fill out the background of his story. It is the method of the **epic**, and a method followed in the twentieth century by Joseph Conrad, who even more than Melville used diversions from the main story as a means of creating suspense and an air of **realism** or believability. In actuality it is rarely if ever that we discover in chronological order the facts surrounding any great event. What usually happens is that we discover them in a disconnected and often incoherent order which we later rearrange into an intelligible pattern.

Among the famous naval personages referred to in Chapter Four are: Don John of Austria, whose fleet defeated the Turks at Lepanto in Greece in 1571, and who numbered among his crewmen Miguel Cervantes, author of Don Quixote; Andrea Doria, the Genoese admiral who liberated Genoa from the Turks; Maarten Tromp, the famous Dutch commander in the struggle of that country with Spain, Portugal and England; Jean Bart, the famous French privateer; and Stephen Decatur, the famous American who fought against the pirates at Tripoli.

Other references include that to Jeremy Bentham (1784-1832), the famous British philosopher and founder of Utilitarianism (a philosophic system which argued that "the greatest happiness of the greatest number is the foundation of morals and legislation"). The Monitor of course is the name of the northern ironclad involved in the famous duel with the Merrimac during the American Civil war.

CHAPTER FIVE

Although the mutiny at Nore had been suppressed, some of the practices against which that mutiny had been directed still existed. For example, the involuntary impressment of seamen, an ancient practice, still continued since it was the only way by which Britain could secure enough men to man her great fleet. Unlike modern vessels which use steam power, sailing ships required the muscle power of many men, a requirement not multiplied beyond the normal because of the war with France.

The great mutinies at Spithead and Nore had not, of course, solved all of the problems of the British seamen. In the period immediately following these mutinies, the British Navy, aware that discontent still existed, took certain actions to prevent a recurrence of the mutinies. In one instance, Vice Admiral Nelson was transferred from the Captain to the Theseus in the hope that his presence aboard that ship would win back the allegiance of the mutineers. In other, less happy circumstances, captains felt it necessary to force their crews to fight under threat of their own officers' swords.

Comment

We are here again reminded that the recent great mutinies remain fresh in the minds of those in command aboard ships of the British fleet.

CHAPTER SIX

Although the fear of recurrent mutiny is general aboard ships of the British fleet, such fear is not evident aboard the Indomitable. Here Captain Edward Fairfax Vere, a sailor of reknown, is in command. A bachelor of forty or so, Captain Vere had served with great distinction under Admiral George Brydges Rodney in the defeat of the French Admiral DeGrasse in the battle of the Leeward Islands in 1732, and as a result of his efforts in that battle, he had been made a captain.

Although Captain Vere did not in general act or look like a famous sailor, the fact remained that he was. A quiet, aristocratic, modest man, he was known to his subordinates as "Starry" Vere because of his habit of gazing dreamily into space, and because Lord Denton, a cousin, had borrowed this description from a poem of Andrew Marvell (1621-1678), in which Marvell had described a famous ancestor of Denton and Vere with the term "Starry." As nicknames will, especially when they are appropriate, the name "Starry" remained permanently attached.

Comment

While he is no Nelson, Captain Vere is a capable and respected officer in spite of his tendency toward dreaminess. This notion of his character is, of course, of great importance later in the story. For although Captain Vere is an intelligent and sensitive man who is not entirely impractical, neither his sensitivity nor his intelligence will restrain him from committing a barbaric act in his summary condemnation of Billy. Nor will these characteristics restrain him from justifying his act by convincing himself that he had followed the only course open to him under the Articles of War.

Symbolically Captain Vere is the flesh and blood representation of all who justify either their action or inability to act by reference to established codes or laws. Although he is sensitive enough to question the justice of the codes under which he acts, he is not capable of challenging them.

CHAPTER SEVEN

Captain Vere was a man of many interests. His years of service at sea had not absorbed all his energies, for on each voyage he had taken with him a carefully replenished library of books. Among his favorites were books of history, biography, and the works of common sense philosophers who sought not to change the world, but to explain it. It was in his reading that he found the satisfaction of intellectual communication which was lacking in the conversation of those who surrounded him. There too, he found the confirmation of his own long held opinions, which were opposed to change and innovation. Though unlike his aristocratic contemporaries who opposed change on the grounds of birth, Captain Vere opposed new ideas because they seemed to him incapable of creating lasting institutions, and were at war with the established institutions and customs.

There were many to whom Captain Vere appeared somewhat dry and bookish, a charge not without some foundation since he unfailingly included some historical or literary reference in his conversation without consideration as to whether or not his often remote references were known to his company.

Comment

This chapter is a good example of Melville's often dry humor. Not only does the chapter adequately describe the pedantic speech of Captain Vere, but it also describes Melville's characteristic mode of composition. There is, however, a significant difference. Melville in *Billy Budd* did not address himself to so limited an audience as did Captain Vere. *Billy Budd*, though understandable to even the most uninformed reader, has within it many levels of meaning which are available to more experienced and sophisticated readers as a result of its many allusions.

Chapter Seven also reveals the paradox of Captain Vere's character. Though he is assuredly a thoroughly competent seaman, and a well-read, intelligent man, he is a man who does not seek to expand the borders of that intelligence, but merely to confirm them. Knowledge is not to him a means of self-expansion. Like so many of his contemporaries his is an unquestioning obedience to the existing order. So much so, in fact, that he cannot conceive of change. Further proof of Captain Vere's belief may be seen in the reference to his favorite philosopher, Michael Montaigne (1533-1592, actually a famous essayist), who believed that man is a being capable of attaining truth. He is only the obedient servant of customs, prejudices, and self-interest; and he is a victim of circumstances and the impressions which circumstances make upon him. These, of course, are the pessimistic beliefs of all who by nature or by reason choose to resist change because they envision all change as evil.

CHAPTER EIGHT

Among the officers and petty officers aboard the Indomitable there is only one who needs to be further described. This is John Claggart, Master-at-arms. Although his title had years before described the function of that office, to instruct the men in the use of arms, sword or cutlass, his present function is the preserving of order on the lower gun deck in the fashion of a policeman.

Claggart was a man about thirty-five, spare and tall, with a high forehead and a heavy chin. His pale complexion suggested that his official duties kept him much out of the sun and contrasted strangely with the deep tan of most of the other sailors. Indeed, there seemed some hint of abnormality about him, for his appearance was more that of a preacher or schoolteacher rather than that of a seaman. Nothing was known of his former life, though a slight accent indicated to some that he was probably not English.

Although the ship was filled with rumors of Claggart's activities before entering the service, and many of the crew believed he had been involved in a great swindle, little was actually known. What was known was that he had entered the Navy comparatively late in life as an ordinary seaman without any previous experience, and had risen rapidly to his present rank. Nor did such rumors spring only from the fact that officers of his rank were generally unpopular with their shipmates.

Impressment officers urgently in need of men to fill ships' complements had often emptied jails, and men in difficulty with the law had discovered in the Navy a convenient refuge. There were, indeed, numerous instances which might be cited to prove the truth of these facts.

Although these speculations about Claggart appeared the result of idle gossip or rumor, the fact was that he had risen rapidly to his present rank through "sobriety, ingratiating deference to his superiors," and a genius for securing information. And now in his present position, with the aid of his corporals, he firmly controlled his subordinates, often to their extreme discomfort, through devious and underground methods.

Comment

The character of Claggart forebodes evil for all who come into contact with him. A strange and austere man, his evil nature appears reflected in his black hair and sallow complexion, like a creature of the underworld. Nor does Melville's comparison of him to Shawnee, an Indian chieftain who joined the British in the War of 1812, and Titus Oates, who organized the plot to assassinate King Charles II in 1678, lessen our awareness of his treacherous character.

Until the middle of the nineteenth century, imprisonment for debt or for mere suspicion of criminal activity was possible in England, and in general, "voluntary" enlistment into the king's service was a customary means of release.

CHAPTER NINE

Life in the foretop agreed with Billy Budd. Here among the exclusive society of those men picked for their youth and strength for his dangerous and difficult job, Billy was able to look down at the busy world of the decks below. He gave no offense to anyone, and he became even more efficient at his duties since he had, the day following his impressment, witnessed a "formal gangplank punishment." On that day a young after-guardsman had been severely whipped for being absent from his post, and Billy, horrified, had resolved never to get into trouble. To his surprise, however, it seemed that he was always in difficulty because his sea bag was not stowed properly or his hammock arranged wrongly, matters controlled by the gun deck corporals under Claggart.

Billy could not understand how these things happened, and when he spoke of them to his foretop mates they simply laughed. There was, however, a veteran sailor aboard, Old Dansker, who had befriended Billy and in whom Billy confided. Dansker, who had served with Nelson aboard the Agamemnon, was a peculiar and eccentric man who did not often make friends among his shipmates, but willingly accepted the proffered friendship of the innocent young man who always treated him with deference and respect. Old Dansker listened quietly to Billy's recital of his troubles and informed Billy in his own characteristic way that "Jemmy Legs is down on you." Meaning, of course, that Baby Budd, as Dansker humorously chose to call Billy, had somehow incurred the enmity of the Master-at-arms. This information, of course, puzzled Billy not a little since in his own guileless and innocent way he had assumed that the Master-at-arms actually liked him. For didn't the Master-at-arms have a pleasant word for him whenever they met? Dansker, refusing further explanation, simply reiterated that the Master-at-arms' pleasant greeting was indeed proof that he was down on Billy, a fact which the young and innocent Billy could in no way comprehend.

Comment

Old Dansker is portrayed as a seer or oracle of old from whom men seek answers to the riddle of life. And he, true to the tradition of all seers and oracles, answers their questions in so direct a fashion that the answer itself proves a puzzle. As a means of reinforcing the impression, Dansker is compared to Merlin, the magician of King Arthur's court, and to Chiron, the wise centaur who befriended Achilles, the hero of Troy. Dansker's use of the term "Jemmy Legs" as a sign of disparagement for "Master-at-arms" is still in use in the United States Navy.

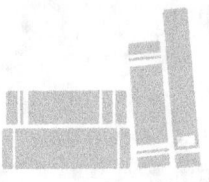

BILLY BUDD

TEXTUAL ANALYSIS

CHAPTERS 10-19

CHAPTER TEN

Like the seekers at the oracles of old, Billy is unable to believe in Dansker's revelation, and the day following his discussion with Dansker an incident occurred which made it even more difficult for Billy to believe in the old seaman's warning.

While Billy was lunching with his mates, the ship gave a sudden lurch and Billy spilled his mess upon a freshly scrubbed deck. Claggart, passing by, was about to ignore the event until he noticed who had spilled the food. He represses a quick retort to the sailor and, instead, points to the streaming soup, tapping him from behind with his rattan and saying melodiously, "Handsomely done, my lad! And handsome is as handsome did it too!" Billy misses the ugly smile of the departing Master-at-arms, and the crew takes his remarks for humor and feels obligated to laugh. Billy also believes the comments are a good-natured sally and joins in the fun. "There now, who says that Jemmy Legs is down on me!" he announces triumphantly and then realizes that this was a foolish utterance since only one person, Dansker, had made mention of it to him.

As Claggart leaves, a drummer-boy bumps into him and is upset over the unguarded hatred in the man's expression. Claggart hits him with his rattan angrily and shouts "Look where you go!"

Comment

Melville's comment that the sailors laughed "with counterfeited glee" at Claggart's remarks, is a quotation borrowed from Oliver Goldsmith's The Deserted Village (1770). In that poem, the oppressed schoolboys are forced to laugh at the jokes of their severe teacher. Melville's **allusion** is effective and links Claggart with another tyrant, of whom Goldsmith says that his subordinates "learned to trace the day's disasters in his morning face."

CHAPTER ELEVEN

"What was the matter with the Master-at-arms?" the narrator inquires and proceeds to discuss the problem. Prior to the soup incident Claggart had never come into contact with the sailor, who was well-known as a peacemaker. Why, then, should he be down on the young man? But down on him he is.

Had there been some earlier encounter between the two one could understand Claggart's present enmity. However there was none. Claggart's hatred, spontaneous and deep, was aroused by the mere presence of harmless Billy. Was this hatred provoked then by Billy's harmlessness? It is all a mystery.

To an average man the tensions aboard ship are such that they can result in frequent quarrels. Hence the need for self-control. But how is Claggart ("some peculiar human creature the direct reverse of a saint") to cope with such conflicts, for Claggart cannot be comprehended by a knowledge of normal human nature. To suggest the complexity of the Master-at-arms, the narrator presents an anecdote. Long ago an educated friend said to him in reference to a mutual acquaintance who, while seemingly respectful, still was inexplicable and a mystery, "Yes, X____ is a nut not to be cracked by the top of a lady's fan," and that "to try and get into X____, enter his labyrinth and get out again, without a clue derived from some source other than what is known as knowledge of the world - that were hardly possible, at least for me."

The narrator protested to him that X____ was yet human and that a knowledge of the world implies a knowledge of human nature. His friend answers that perhaps "to know the world and to know human nature be not two distinct branches of knowledge, which while they may coexist in the same heart, yet either may exist with little or nothing of the other." Perhaps with most people an ability to perceive the true nature of exceptional characters, whether good or bad, becomes stunted in the course of time. He knew a girl once who had gotten around an accomplished lawyer because "he knew law better than he knew the girl's heart."

The narrator feels that his friend's examples can be readily applied to Claggart. Although scripture might explain the evil nature of Claggart, unfortunately few are willing to accept its worth today, so other authorities will have to be cited. He then offers Plato's definition: "Natural Depravity: a depravity according to nature," and feels that this might apply to certain rare individuals, such as Claggart. Such a type of person often bears a refinement and a developed intellect which is not found among the petty and brute criminals. This sort possesses an unusual pride which will not permit him to be compromised by anything vulgar or greedy. Nothing sensual, low, or bitter is embodied in the depravity, and as a result by excluding minor vices he creates a facade of respectability and decorum which permits him access to civilized society.

Though it would seem that such a person would be most rational, nothing could be farther from the truth, for his heart is completely detached from the faculty of reason and only employs reason as an instrument to effect the heart's most irrational and destructive purposes. "Toward the accomplishment of an aim which in wantonness of malignity would seem to partake of the insane, he will direct a cool judgment, sagacious and sound."

These are the true lunatics and of the most potentially dangerous variety for their madness is not continuous (which could be easily noticed and checked), but occasional (which can pass undetected) and always evoked by some special object. So hidden and self-contained is it, that while it is most active to all outward appearances, such a person seems totally sane and normal. Nor are the aims and the secret sources of their sickness understood or communicated, for all their external actions seem perfectly normal and rational.

This then is the narrator's view of Claggart. This is all he knows that can possibly help to shed light on his strange behavior. The evil nature of Claggart is not the result of a cruel education or environment or the product of decadent reading or licentiousness, but is innate, "a depravity according to nature."

Comment

Melville writes that there is the quality of the mysterious present here similar to that in the celebrated Gothic romance, The Mysteries of Udolpho (1794), by Ann Radcliffe, who specialized in stimulating terror in her readers. Melville is thus broadening our understanding of Claggart by suggesting his connection with the supernatural and horrifying elements of Gothic fiction.

It is significant that the narrator tells us that neither Sir Edward Coke (an English judge and writer on law, 1552-1634) nor Sir William Blackstone (an English legal writer and judge, 1723-80) has "hardly shed so much light into obscure places as the Hebrew prophets." He thus reinforces the earlier comment that there was a great gap between knowledge of the world and knowledge of human nature. How little these judges knew as compared with that profound knowledge of evil and human nature which the ancient prophets possessed.

While quoting Plato's term 'natural depravity,' the narrator reveals its relationship to Calvinism. John Calvin (1509-1564) was a French Protestant theologian who preached a doctrine of predestination which argued that God has already determined who will be rewarded in Heaven or damned to Hell prior to the person's birth into this world. Thus Plato's 'natural depravity' and Calvin's predestination both imply an arbitrary sentencing which totally excludes any choice or free will by man, with the result that a man is not then responsible for his evil condition in either instance, and cannot be held truly guilty or accountable for his evil nature. Thus the entire chapter reflects Melville's career-long obsession with the problem of evil in the universe.

CHAPTER TWELVE

The narrator digresses. Could it be that the phenomenon of natural depravity is the hidden motivation eluding those attending to criminal trials? Both lawyers and physicians claim to present expert evidence, yet differ and quarrel among themselves. The narrator suggests that pastors be subpoenaed as well. Since their vocation brings them into contact with so many varied types of human nature, and they are privy to the most intimate and startling revelations, they would be most qualified to present valuable testimony to the intricate problems of moral responsibility. They could help determine, in certain instances, whether "the crime proceeded from mania in the brain or rabies of the heart." Even if they were to disagree among themselves they would be less contentious than the medical doctors because it is well supposed that they would be free from the possibilities of being corrupted by bribes.

Comment

The narrator again complains that so few today are willing to be guided or instructed by Holy Writ. He refers to Paul's second epistle to the Thessalonians (ii:7) which discourses on the presence of evil in the affairs of the world, and reinforces his own interpretation of Claggart's behavior which suggests the "mysteries of iniquity." He thus forces us to turn from mere psychological and scientific explanations to a study of theology in order to come to grips with the character of Claggart, and by doing so, he adds a religious dimension to the story and another topic to ponder in our comprehension of it.

This chapter is relevant and no mere space filler, for the insistence of a "clerical proficient" to be present at a trial anticipates the actual trial of Billy Budd later on in the story, where no minister is in attendance and, by inference, no religious point of view is presented, only the less than divine legal and martial particulars.

CHAPTER THIRTEEN

Carefully dressed and meticulous in his person, Claggart presented an attractive appearance, but he was pale beside the heroic form of Billy. And Billy, though not as intellectually intense as the Master-at-arms, far more than compensates by his fine virtue: "The bonfire in his heart made luminous the rose-tan in his check." It is thus this contrast between the two which provides the clue to the ultimate nature of Claggart's hatred. Claggart's "handsome is as handsome does" revealed clearly what had first turned him against the foretopman, namely, "his significant personal beauty."

To a rational person the passions of envy and repugnance are irreconcilable, but in such a temperament as Claggart's, they may be conjoined like the Siamese Twins, Chang and Eng (1811-1874). Envy is a most unpleasant failing. Who would have his prestige harmed by owning up to such an ugly and hideous trait? Since it is seated in man's heart and not his brain, no degree of intellectual development can ward if off. But Claggart's envy is deep, for Billy's good looks and happy disposition reflect an innocent spirit devoid of malice and evil

- the exact antithesis of his own soul. The term "the handsome sailor" sums up all that is noble and pure in Billy, a spiritual quality dimly recognized by all who know him, and most especially later by Captain Vere.

Thus while sneering at innocence, Claggart instinctively perceives Billy's moral superiority. He, too, would have liked to possess Billy's natural goodness and charm though despairing of any possible moral improvement. A nature such as Claggart's "apprehending the good, but powerless to be it," readies its thwarted energies and like the scorpion he can do naught but "act out to the end the part allotted it."

Comment

Melville is here in the mainstream of the Romantic tradition. The uneducated, simple Billy possesses far greater spirituality and humanity than any intellectual might own. He is the concrete example of the superiority of the 'noble savage' to the sophisticated urbanite.

By using a line from Book IV of Milton's *Paradise Lost* (1.115) as a chapter heading, Melville reintroduces the Adam **theme**. (In Chapter Two he had already described Billy as "a sort of upright barbarian, much such perhaps as Adam might presumably have been ere the urbane serpent wriggled himself into his company.") The quoted phrase sets the mood and suggests a parallel with Milton's work. In Book IV Satan remarks as he sets out to discover (and later destroy) God's new and perfect creation, Man, "All good to me is lost, Evil, be thou my good." Milton continues: "Thus while he spake, each passion dimmed his face,

Thrice changed with pale-ire, envy, and despair; Which marred his borrowed visage, and betrayed Him, counterfeit, if any eye beheld: For heavenly minds from such distempers foul Are ever clear."

Thus the story of the serpent in the Garden of Eden is retold. Billy is himself that unspoiled Adam, who remains innocently unaware of the evil and destructive mission of Claggart.

Claggart's envy of Billy is profounder than "that streak of apprehensive jealousy that marred Saul's visage perturbedly brooding on the comely young David," another significant Biblical **allusion**. Saul had only slain thousands, but David had killed "his ten thousands" (I Samuel xviii: 6-13). Subsequently he becomes greatly displeased and, in his envy, tries to kill David twice with a javelin. The reference is apt, for Claggart is very similar to Saul: "the evil spirit from God came upon Saul." Besides enriching the narrative, these frequent Biblical quotations stretch the meanings and possible interpretations of the narrative.

It is interesting to note that the destructive actions of both Claggart and the scorpion to which he is compared appear predetermined.

CHAPTER FOURTEEN

Profound passion needs no grandiose stage to be enacted. At present the gun deck of the Indomitable can be the setting, and the spilling of a man's soup can serve as the incident which triggers tragedy.

When Claggart noticed the streaming soup he immediately thought, perhaps willed the thought, that this was a deliberate action on Billy's part to demonstrate his hatred for him. The Master-at-arms, blinded by envy, cannot see that it was a mere accident, and a poisonous hatred is quickly aroused in his heart. This event vindicates the reports of Squeak, a rodent-like corporal, who, sensing the Master-at-arm's loathing of Billy, is not above distorting the youth's innocuous remarks to make it appear that the foretopman hates Claggart and ridicules him openly to his mates. This is the same sailor who has been harassing Billy by untidying his hammock under instructions from Claggart, and the Master-at-arms, knowing of his own unpopularity with the men, who privately mocked him, willingly believed all the smears and lies which Squeak related to him concerning Billy.

Claggart did not really need such a toad as Squeak to inflame his passion. Along with his depraved nature went a heightened prudence, for there was so much to conceal from the world. At the slightest insult or apparent injury, he would swiftly recoil from examining the possible offense objectively, and inwardly brood on the matter until he could contain the thirst for vengeance no longer and retaliate with ferocity far more severe than was necessary to avenge a wrong. Although Claggart has a conscience, it is under the control of his will, which like a lawyer, serves only to try to condemn Billy and, from the limited evidence of the soup spilling and the supposed name calling, to prove conclusively that Billy was beyond a doubt guilty. Thus his conscience justifies his hatred, and gives him the right to strike back and punish with impunity. Although the earlier secret persecutions of Billy were carried out to test him or provoke him, it was the event of the soup-spilling which gave Claggart the excuse he was looking for, and he could now continue his persecutions self-righteously.

Comment

Not without significance do the opening lines suggest the drama, for Melville is calling to mind Greek Tragedy. How appropriately Billy Budd fits into such a designation: the noble hero with a tragic flaw (Billy's stuttering); the unities of time, place and action (the events occur within a brief span of time and within the confines of one ship; there are no sub-plots, etc.). The successful drama, opera, and film adaptations, of course, realize the dramatic elements inherent in the novel.

Squeak is another obvious example of Melville's tendency to give names to characters which indicate their natures. Squeak is an informer whose name conveys well his resemblance to a rodent. Billy Budd is in the 'bud' of youth; Captain Vere represents Truth (his name in Latin means 'the true'), at least as far as this world knows Truth.

Among the many clues which Melville gives to Claggart's character is the reference to the Pharisee. "The Pearisee is the Guy Fawkes prowling in the hid chambers underlying the Claggarts." The Pharisees were an ancient Jewish sect noted for strict observance of the law without regard for its spirit. Such an outward show of morality led them to pretensions of superior sanctity and self-righteousness. Guy Fawkes (1570-1606) was an English conspirator, one of the leaders of the Gunpowder Plot (1604-1605) to blow up the Houses of Parliament. Thus, these two references underline the hypocrisy and the potential violence of such a man as Claggart.

CHAPTER FIFTEEN

Soon after the incident of the soup, a much more upsetting event takes place. While sleeping on the uppermost deck near the foremast on a warm night, Billy is awakened by a voice which quietly urges him to meet him in the lee forechains, "There is something in the wind."

Although still drowsy, the foretopman is unable to say no to any rational request, and although he wonders what could be in the wind, he goes to the designated spot which is one of the most secluded places on the Indomitable. There the stranger joins him, and though there is a haze and no moon, Billy recognizes him from his outline as one of the afterguardsmen.

The man whispers, "You were impressed, weren't you? Well, so was I." When Billy doesn't answer, the man tells him that they aren't the only impressed men on board. "There's a gang of us. - Couldn't you-help-at a pinch?" Billy, now fully awake, demands a further explanation and the afterguard offers some coins to Billy to bribe him into joining an insurrection. Billy responds with such anger that he stutters. He doesn't know what the man is driving at, but tells him that he had better go back where he belongs. When the fellow doesn't move, Billy springs to his feet and threatens to toss him overboard and the afterguard flees.

The commotion rouses the forecastleman and he shouts "What's the matter?" Billy calms down, controls his stammer, and announces that he had discovered an afterguardsman in his section of the ship and that he had bid him be off. Red Pepper, the forecastleman's associate, replies that he would not have let the man off so lightly, for trespassing by the afterguardsmen is bitterly resented by the forecastlemen. Nonetheless, Billy's account satisfies the inquiring forecastlemen.

CHAPTER SIXTEEN

This incident disturbed Billy. Never before had he been approached in so underhanded a manner. Up to now he knew nothing about the afterguardsman. What did it all mean? Were they genuine guineas which had been held up to his eyes? Where could the sailor have obtained so much money? Sensing that it involved evil of some sort, Billy became more discomfited as he pondered the puzzling event. Though curious to see what the afterguardsman would look like in the daytime, he had no desire to inquire further into the matter, recoiling as if by instinct from any questionable conspiracies.

The next afternoon Billy catches sight of the man and recognizes him. Could it be he, this fellow about his own age, laughing with his mates, a chubby sailor who did not appear too bright, who was planning a revolt. The afterguardsman notices Billy's stare and nods to him familiarly without interrupting his conversation. They chance to meet soon again and the sailor greets him with a "flying word of good-fellowship" which come so unexpectedly and with such doubtful intent that Billy is embarrassed and cannot respond.

Billy cannot understand these events. The more he tries to think them out, the more upset he becomes. In his attempt to forget it, it does not occur to him that he is obliged to report such mutinous matters to the authorities. Had he thought of doing it, he would have undoubtedly restrained the urge since he would not tattle on a fellow sailor.

Finally one calm night, while sitting with Dansker on the deck, the desire comes over Billy to unburden himself of his disquieting thoughts to his experienced and mature ally. Not wanting to tell everything and so be known as a tattler, Billy discusses the events of that mysterious evening in a general way without referring to the afterguardsman by name. Dansker sees through the foretopman's account and senses more than he has been told. And after mediating for a while, he says with assurance, "Didn't I say so, Baby Budd?" When Billy does not understand, Dansker announces, "Why, Jemmy Legs is down on you." And Billy, in amazement, asks what Claggart has to do with the afterguardsman. Thus, in this confusion, he inadvertently lets slip who the conspirator was.

"Ho, it was an afterguardsman then. A cat's paw, a cat's paw," exclaims Dansker, and, with that, bites into his tobacco plug, and in spite of Billy's repeated queries, the old sailor remains silent. Years at sea have taught him caution-neither to interfere in anything nor to give advice.

Comment

To reinforce our view that Billy is totally innocent, Melville compares his reaction to the underhanded activities of the afterguardsman to "a young horse fresh from the pasture suddenly inhaling a vile whiff from some chemical factory and by repeated snortings tries to get it out of his nostrils and lungs." Billy, like the young horse, is unable to cope with a corrupt civilization (one decaying and hence offensive to the sense of smell), because both are in a supreme state of natural purity and innocence.

As in Chapter Nine Melville repeats the earlier hint that Dansker's comments are "oracular," coming as if from the "Delphic deliverances" of old. Stated as riddles, these were either unclear or capable of more than one interpretation. Dansker is also referred to as "old Merlin," a magician as well as a seer to King Arthur. Thus Dansker's concluding statement is in the nature of an oracular deliverance, for "cat's paw" is a nautical term describing a light breeze which ruffles the surface of the water over a relatively small area, and is also a figure of speech which implies that a person is being used by another to serve his purposes. Finally, a "cat's paw" is a type of hitch in the angle of a rope, made to hook a tackle on. Unfortunately these figurative meanings elude Billy, for he cannot realize that Dansker is inferring that the afterguardsman is one of Claggart's henchmen and is attempting to trap him. Although this "cat's paw" may not be a serious "storm," but only a "breeze," Billy is warned to be on his guard and beware of the Master-at-arms' snares.

CHAPTER SEVENTEEN

Despite Dansker's warnings, Billy still cannot agree that Claggart is "down on him." The foretopman still regards him as one who "always had a pleasant word for him." What seems obvious to wise old Dansker is beyond the grasp of young Billy, who remains a "child-man" at heart. Though the average person loses his innocence as he gains intelligence, it is not so with Billy, for his mental growth has in no way affected his innocent, trusting heart. In brief, Billy is almost totally lacking in worldly experience.

"And what could Billy know of man except of man as a mere sailor?" the narrator asks. The only men he knew were his fellow sailors, sailors who as a group are different from men who live on land. Men on land tend to be sophisticated; men at sea are more likely to be naive, "a juvenile race." Moreover, the sailors in Billy's time had few personal responsibilities. Accustomed only to obeying orders instantly, their lives were fixed and ruled. And even when they rebelled, they misbehaved in a juvenile way. In a sense these sailors were so protected that they could only deal with each other in an open, friendly way. Unfortunately this cannot be said about men who do not live at sea. On land if men should go about trusting everyone and being friendly, they should soon be duped and taken advantage of. Hence, men learn to conceal their feelings and form the habits of caution and suspicion.

Comment

Melville adds to our knowledge of the virtue of the foretopman: "he had none of that intuitive knowledge of the bad." This is not an ideal condition to be in, for from the comments which follow, we can see that Billy, incapable by nature of recognizing potential harm, is totally unprepared to cope with it when it happens. Unlike sophisticated men of the world, and blind to evil, he is easily victimized by Claggart.

Melville inserted a small set piece in this chapter on the meaninglessness and pettiness of most of the activities in this world (a theme which occupied him throughout his career): "Life is not a game with the sailor, demanding the long head; no intricate game of chess where few moves are made in straightforwardness, and ends are attained by indirection; an oblique, tedious, barren game hardly worth that poor candle burnt out in playing it." This last line recalls a famous quotation from the Essays of Michel de Montaigne (1533-1592), "The game is not worth the candle," as well as Shakespeare's pessimistic speech, spoken by Macbeth, "Out, out, brief candle. Life's but a walking shadow, a poor player That struts and frets his hour upon the stage, And then is heard no more; it is a tale Told by an idiot, full of sound and fury, Signifying nothing." (Macbeth, Act V, Scene 5, 11. 23-27)

CHAPTER EIGHTEEN

After the soup-spilling incident (Chapter 14), Billy finds that he has no more problems with disorderly hammocks or clothes bags. Even Claggart's smiles and greetings to him have become more frequent and more charming. However, unnoticed by the foretopman, the Master-at-arms occasionally catches the happy youth chatting with his friends at leisure time and stares at him "with a settled meditative and melancholy expression." At these times his eyes would slowly fill with tears and he would "look like the man of sorrows," and there would be something of an impossible yearning in this sad expression as if Claggart would have loved Billy if it weren't for fate and the curse invoked upon his soul. These tender feeling are however brief, quickly regretted, and soon replaced by a hard glare which shrivels Claggart's face into the resemblance "of a wrinkled walnut."

Although many innocent people have an instinct which warns them to beware when they are in the presence of evil, Billy lacks even this ability. Aware of Claggart's strange looks, he's incapable of comprehending their purpose. He regards these actions as rather odd and lets it go at that. Claggart's seemingly pleasant exchanges he takes at face value and misses completely their underlying hatred. Had Billy consciously said or done anything to incur the enmity of Claggart, he might immediately understand the Master-at-arms' bitter expressions. As it is, "innocence was his blinder."

In addition to Claggart, two minor officers, the Armorer and the Captain of the Hold, begin to give the "Handsome Sailor" peculiar examining looks, and though Billy knows that these two men are mess-mates of Claggart's, he is not the least bit suspicious, but rather takes comfort in the fact that he is well liked by most of his shipmates.

Well liked he is, for his manliness and good nature endear him to almost everyone. And since he has not the mental superiority to make anyone envious, why should he trouble himself with the odd stares of a few? Even the afterguardsman seems to have dropped all sinister mannerisms and now treats him in a friendly fashion.

It would seem that for once Claggart's highly developed evil instincts have deceived him, for the man he sought to trap does not respond to his provocations. In this innocent ignorance, Billy has managed to avoid all entanglements with the scheming Master-at-arms. Although a sharp observer may question why Billy does not meet the afterguardsman straight on and demand to know the meaning of the secret interview or at least discover for himself the truth to the notion that the impressed men are planning a revolt, such objections are pointless, for they fail to grasp Billy's simple and unusual character.

Meanwhile Claggart remains obsessed with one goal: he will not permit Billy to escape his evil intentions. Like insanity, his passion is involuntary, springing from his depraved nature, yet one which can be concealed under a controlled and rational demeanor. His madness, "like a subterranean fire was eating its way deeper and deeper in him," and must be quenched as quickly as possible.

Comment

Melville describes Billy as "the cheerful sea-Hyperion," one who excites melancholy for a brief instant in Claggart. In early Greek mythology Hyperion was a Titan who was the father of the sun, the moon, and the dawn. In later Greek and Roman mythology he was identified with Apollo, the god of light, health, and music, and thus represented the highest type of youthful, manly beauty.

Claggart, seeing Billy near, readies a crooked smile which is compared to "the glittering dental **satire** of a Guise." Here, one recalls Hamlet who, learning of his Uncle Claudius' treachery, proclaims: "O villain, smiling, damned villain! Than one way smile, and smile, and be a villain" (Hamlet, Act I, 11. 106, 108). In addition the Guises were a powerful ducal family in France (sixteenth and seventeenth centuries) who were active in violent intrigues.

So cunning and villainous is Claggart, that should he be interrupted in his staring at Billy with malice by any unforeseen encounter "a red light would forth from his eye like a spark from an anvil in a dusk smithy." His defense mechanism thus suggests a powerful instinct for concealment, such as vicious animals, or even Satan himself, might possess.

Melville has masterfully succeeded in creating great suspense and tension with these brief incidents and asides, and now the reader is prepared for the exciting climax.

CHAPTER NINETEEN

Because of a shortage of suitable ships, the Indomitable is used at times as a shouting vessel, and for even more important tasks considering the superior capability of its commander. During one of these scouting missions, the ship catches sight of an enemy frigate, chases it for a lengthy time, but finally loses sight of it. Shortly afterward when the excitement dies down, Claggart stands near the mainmast and, removing his cap, waits to catch the attention of Captain Vere who is pacing the quarterdeck, annoyed by the enemy ship's escape. The Master-at-arms is standing on the spot assigned to men of lesser grades who seek an interview with their superiors. For him to request a hearing with the Captain himself is not unusual.

Finally the Captain notices Claggart and although he knows the petty officer only slightly because the man has only been on the ship since the Indomitable's last sailing from home, a strange expression comes over his face as if he were observing Claggart for the first time, not just quickly as before, and is suddenly filled with a "vaguely repellent distaste." Standing in an official manner, he asks Claggart somewhat impatiently what is the matter.

Claggart assumes the air of one who is upset at bearing bad news and though anxious to be frank, feels the need to shun overstatement. He announces in a refined and roundabout way that during the chase and preparations for combat he has seen enough to make him positive that there is at least one dangerous sailor aboard who is organizing his fellow impressed seamen and some of those guilty of earlier mutiny. He has suspected that these activities were secretly conducted on the gun decks but had refrained from reporting until he had sufficient evidence as to the man's guilt. Claggart then adds that he is aware of the serious responsibility which he has assumed in making this report which may have grievous consequences to the party concerned. He regrets, too, that the anxieties of the captain must be increased, beset as he is now with the problem of the recent mutinies.

Captain Vere conceals his surprise at his upset from Claggart. Although he grows restless, he allows the ma to continue. However, when the Master-at-arms begins to say that he wishes the Indomitable to avoid the fate of the Nore Mutiny, the Captain interrupts his mention of that dread affair. How dare the man presume to bring up such unpleasant matters in his presence?

The Captain quickly regains his composure. After all, he must listen to this attempt to warn him, and he ponders whether the Master-at-arms, so tactful before, would be deliberately tactless now unless for a serious cause. Yet with such long experience at sea the captain will not permit himself to be disturbed unnecessarily, though it may be that prompt action must be taken. Still he disapproves of the informer's tactics, and does not wish to have the reputation of spying on his men in a policelike way. In any case, the Captain is not sympathetic toward Claggart. The man's earlier forced zeal had struck the Captain as false, and his manner now reminds him of a perjurous witness at a court-martial of which he had been a member.

The Captain quickly asks who this "dangerous man might be" and when Claggart mentions Billy's name, the amazed Captain asks if this be not the same handsome sailor impressed by Lieutenant Ratcliffe. Claggart says he is but goes on to point out that Billy made friends only so that they could defend him if he ever got caught, and argues that Billy's good-humored arrival aboard the ship only covered his hatred of being an impressed seaman. He concludes that Billy is a potentially dangerous man.

The Captain, however, thinks otherwise and sees no sinister motive behind Billy's actions. In fact, Billy has been so adept that he has considered promoting him to the captaincy of the mizzentop to replace a less fit sailor. In short, Billy seems to be a "King's bargain," one who returns great service for the small amount of effort in procuring him. Thus reaffirming his convictions as to Billy's worth, Captain Vere doubts the slurs he has just heard and says, "Do you come to me, Master-at-arms, with so foggy a tale?" Demanding actual proof, he orders Claggart to confirm his statements by referring to words spoken or to definite acts performed, first warning him of the punishment which befalls those who bear false witness. Indignant because the Captain fails to take his charges seriously, Claggart stands erect in a posture of self-assertion and circumstantially alleges certain statements and actions which, if proved, can convict Billy, and he claims to have sufficient proof to convince the Captain of Billy's guilt. As Captain Vere tries to penetrate Claggart's calm eyes, he hears him out, and ponders the matter. Claggart inspects his face to learn the reaction to his words much like that "of the spokesman of the envious children of Jacob deceptively imposing upon the troubled patriarch."

Captain Vere suspects the Master-at-arms and is filled with odd doubts. He is troubled, not by how to deal with Billy, but more by how best to act toward the informer. If he should call for immediate evidence, this news might affect the morale of the ship, but if Claggart were a false witness then the matter would be ended. So it seemed the ideal thing to test the accuser quietly without public knowledge. Since his long conversation was already beginning to attract attention, he decided to conduct this interview elsewhere. He summons Albert, his trusted sea-valet, and tells him to bring Billy Budd to him, insisting also that Billy talk to no one and be ignorant of his destination until he reaches the present area. Here he is to be told to come to the Captain's cabin.

Comment

The Adam **theme** is repeated, this time by Captain Vere who considers that Billy "in the nude might have posed for a statue of young Adam before the Fall." And it is this chapter as well as others which cause some critics to see Billy as a Christ figure. As the innocent Christ had resisted the temptations of Satan, the innocent Billy has resisted Claggart's attempt at bribery. As the betrayed Christ was falsely accused of refusing to honor the Emperor, Billy is unjustly accused of being disloyal to the King. Only through treachery can both innocent men be brought to trial for the same offense, treason.

Besides resembling Judas Iscariot betraying Christ, Claggart in this chapter resembles Satan as well. As it was Satan who tempted Adam with the sins of rebellion and disobedience, Claggart has tempted Billy with these crimes as well, and though free from guilt (unlike Adam), the foretopman is now falsely accused of them.

BILLY BUDD

TEXTUAL ANALYSIS

CHAPTERS 20-27

CHAPTER TWENTY

When Billy finds himself in a private conference with Claggart and the Captain, he is surprised, but thinks perhaps he is getting a promotion, for his honest, simple nature cannot sense any hint of danger.

The Captain gives orders that the cabin door be closed and they are not to be disturbed. He then tells Claggart to repeat to Billy's face what he had previously related to him so that he may examine the mutually confronting faces. At this command, just as a physician in an insane asylum approaches a patient on the verge of a violent outburst, Claggart advances in a self-controlled and calm manner toward the foretopman, and "mesmerically looking him in the eye," quickly repeats the accusation.

Billy at first does not understand what he hears, but when he does, the rose tan of his cheek looks "struck as by white leprosy." Claggart's eyes change from a rich violet to a muddy purple and lose all human expression, resembling the cold states of some undersea creature.

"Speak, defend yourself," demands the Captain, amazed at such a vile accusation hurled at the inexperienced youth. Unfortunately, Billy is so upset he can only gesture dumbly and utter strange gurgling sounds. A horror of Claggart intensifies his speech defect into a tongue-tied convulsion while the rest of his body strains forward in agony to obey the Captain's command to speak and defend himself. His efforts are pitifully ineffectual and his face registers such pain as to recall "a condemned Vestal priestess in the moment of being buried alive, and in the first struggle against suffocation."

Though prior to this time Captain Vere has been unaware of the foretopman's vocal defect, he senses it quickly for he recalls a young schoolmate who had a similar problem in an emotional crisis. Going to Billy, he lays a comforting hand on his shoulder, and tells him there is no rush, but to take his time. Instead of soothing him however, these fatherly words "Doubtless touching Billy's heart to the quick," make it even more difficult for him to speak. These unsuccessful efforts only serve to confirm his paralysis, and in the next instant, "quick as the flame from a discharged cannon at night, [Billy's] right arm shot out, and Claggart dropped to the deck," gasped and "lay motionless."

"Fated boy," breathes Captain Vere, "what have you done." The two raise Claggart to a sitting position but discover that his body is lifeless. The Captain then covers his face meditatively and when he removes his hand he has altered his expression from a fatherly regard toward Billy to the stern look of a military disciplinarian. In an official manner he bids Billy retire to the stateroom aft and stay there until called for. Billy obeys silently.

Captain Vere sends Albert to summon the Surgeon to the cabin. He arrives quickly and is started to see thick black blood oozing from the protrate Master-at-arms' nose and ear. Although Vere is sure the man is dead, he wants the physician to verify it. Suddenly Captain Vere catches the Surgeon's arm violently and proclaims, "It is the divine judgment on Ananias," an unexpected outburst which disturbs the Surgeon who has never seen the Captain in such a state, and adds to his puzzlement over Claggart's sudden death. For a moment Captain Vere remains motionless. Then swiftly he exclaims vehemently, "Struck dead by an angel of God! Yet the angel must hang!" Finally collecting himself, he proceeds to explain the occurrence to the troubled surgeon, and together they remove the body from sight. Although the Surgeon is upset when the captain orders him to keep his knowledge of the death a secret, and to tell what has happened only to the lieutenants and Mr. Mordant, the captain of marines, who are also charged to keep the matter to themselves, he is forced to obey.

Comment

Claggart is here referred to as Satan, the serpent in the Garden of Eden. When he encounters the foretopman to bring charges against him, his "first mesmeric glance was of serpent fascination," and when the Captain and Billy attempt to pick up the deceased Master-at-arms, we are told that "it was like handling a dead snake." And in another Biblical **allusion** Billy's failure to defend himself from Claggart's accusations recalls the silence of Jesus Christ during the interview between the priests and the elders. Significantly too, we are reminded that Billy's painful effort to speak "was a crucifixion to behold."

Although Billy is perfect in the innocence of his heart, he is touched nonetheless with some elemental imperfection of humanity. His stutter can be seen as a symbol of this (a sort of taint of original sin) and there is a strange justice in the fact that this stutter is his undoing. It is important to note that Captain Vere addresses Billy after he hits Claggart as "fated boy."

"The divine judgment on Ananias" is a reference to an event in the New Testament. Here Ananias is accused by St. Peter of lying to the Holy Ghost: "thou has not lied unto men, but unto God" (Acts v:4-5), whereupon Ananias was struck dead. Nor is Claggart's ugly death unlike that of another betrayer, Judas Iscariot.

CHAPTER TWENTY-ONE

As the Surgeon, full of misgivings, left the cabin, he wondered whether Captain Vere was suddenly affected in his mind or whether this was just a temporary excitement caused by the unusual murder. The drum-head court struck him as completely inexpedient. What should be done, he felt, was to confine Billy in the usual manner and postpone action on this extraordinary event until such time when they should rejoin the squadron, then place the case in the hands of the Admiral.

For a man so normally calm, Captain Vere's agitations and excited exclamations struck the Surgeon as puzzling. Was the man mentally unsound? If so it would be quite difficult to prove it. What was he to do? It is indeed a trying situation for an officer to be subordinate to a Captain whom he suspects of being, if not mad, at least mentally disturbed. Should the Surgeon argue against the Captain's order, it would be insolence; should he resist it, it would be mutiny.

Obeying the Captain's wishes, he informed the lieutenants and captain of marines of Captain Vere's orders but said nothing of the man's state of mind. They shared his own surprise and concern and, like him, thought that such a delicate situation should be referred to the Admiral instead of the Captain's own drum-head court.

Comment

This chapter has the important function of making the reader see that the forthcoming trial and execution of Billy Budd is altogether unnecessary. A sound alternative course of action is suggested, and the reader is thus forewarned that he should not be in complete agreement with the decisions and views of Captain Vere, but that the man's actions and comments are henceforth open for close scrutiny, criticism, and evaluation.

CHAPTER TWENTY-TWO

To draw an exact line between sanity and insanity in a doubtful situation is all but impossible. Whether Captain Vere was the sudden victim of a seizure, as the surgeon thinks, is left to the reader to decide as he judges the former's subsequent actions.

This was a most unfortunate time for such an event to take place, following, as it did, suppressed insurrections and severe criticism of naval authority. Ironically, from a legal point of view, the roles of Billy and Claggart are reversed and the villain seems an innocent victim, while the virtuous foretopman is guilty of the most terrible of naval crimes, the slaying of a superior officer. And now the Captain must judge the events solely from a military viewpoint and not from a basic standard of right and wrong.

Because Captain Vere felt that he must act not only promptly but with extreme caution, he thought it best to keep the matter secret until it was settled conclusively. Unfortunately the net of absolute secrecy surrounding the issues was regarded by many afterwards as an operation resembling the intrigues of foreign courts.

Although he would have preferred keeping Billy a prisoner until he could be turned over to the Admiral, nonetheless, Captain Vere felt that he must obey his "vows of allegiance to martial duty," for unless quick action were to be taken, the news of Billy's deed might spread and incite the crew to possible mutiny. This urgency overrode every other consideration, and the captain, not wishing to take the full responsibility and authority for Billy's trial upon himself, thought it best to turn the matter over to a summary court of his own officers.

A drum-head court was convened, comprising the First Lieutenant, the Captain of marines, and the Sailing Master. Although it was not generally the custom to have an officer of marines for such a procedure, Captain Vere felt that he was capable and trustworthy though perhaps not as adept in solving moral dilemmas as fighting in battles. The other two likewise were more able as seamen than as men of trained intellect for such a difficult responsibility as a drum-head court.

The trial was held in the captain's quarters, two rooms of which served as a jail for Billy and as a resting place for Claggart.

Here Captain Vere was the only witness. Standing in a position worthy of his rank, he gave a concise account of the events leading up to and including the catastrophe, without omitting any details. The three men were shocked to learn what the harmless foretopman had done, but when Billy was questioned as to the truth of the Captain's testimony, he answered, "Captain Vere tells the truth," and reaffirmed his own loyalty to the King. Captain Vere replied to this with controlled emotion, "I believe you, my man." When asked if there were any malice between him and Claggart, Billy replied that he never bore malice against the Master-at-arms. He regrets having killed him and says that he had no intention of hurting him. "Could I have used my tongue I would not have struck him," but because Claggart had lied to his face in the Captain's presence, "I had to say something, and I could only say it with a blow' God help me."

The court at last comprehends the events and Captain Vere repeats, "I believe you, my man." The foretopman is asked if he knew of any plans of mutiny on the ship, and when Billy hesitates, they think it is due to his speech impediment. Though Billy recalls the incident with the afterguardsman, his honor prevents him from being an informer, so he answers "no."

The Officer of the marines then wants Billy to tell him why Claggart should have acted so maliciously since there was no malice between them. The "Handsome Sailor," totally confused, cannot provide an explanation, and he appeals to his friend, Captain Vere, with a beseeching glance. The Captain announces that though the question is perfectly natural, how can Billy or anyone else for that matter answer it. The mystery lies with the deceased man, he reminds the court. A martial court is not concerned with the motivations but solely with the consequences of the blow and the person who struck the blow. The coldness of these remarks upsets Billy and the other men who feel that

Captain Vere has already prejudged the youth, thus increasing their belief in the man's mental disturbance.

Captain Vere in a glance to the First Lieutenant now infers that the proceedings are finished and that he should bring the investigation to a close. And Billy, feeling that silence is now best, replies "I have said all, Sir."

As the foretopman is escorted back to his confinement, the three officers, full of troubled indecision, feel that they must decide and without delay. Brooding on the matter, the Captain paces the cabin floor, then stands before them. He scans their faces and deliberates how best to address these good but intellectually undeveloped men for whom one must demonstrate principles which he himself had always taken for granted. His speech reflects his vast education, an education which some of his men thought he was inclined at times to show off, although they respected his efficiency. He argues that he must assist them in making their decision. Scruples, he tells them, should be put aside in this very special case. They are here not to act as specialists in ethics or moralists, but as practical jurors dealing with martial law. It is not so that the Master-at-arms' death is a capital crime, one that requires the most severe penalty, he asks. Though in natural justice it is shameful for an innocent man to suffer death, he reminds them that their allegiance is not to nature, but to the King. When they became officers, they ceased being natural free agents, but became men forced to obey the call of duty. When war is declared they are not consulted, but fight at command whether or not their judgments approve of the war. Should they decide to condemn Billy, it is not they who are condemning but the martial law which operates through them, a law which they are not responsible for, but have the responsibility of administering. They must not, he tells them, be sentimental about Billy, "let not warm hearts betray heads that should be cool." Would a judge on land permit himself to be swayed by a woman's plea for the defendant?" Then Captain Vere, noticing their doubtful expressions, remarks that they should not place their private consciences over the demands of the martial code. The men remain bothered still and the Captain begins in a more forceful tone to explain that Billy's blow, coming as it did in wartime, is a capital crime under the Articles of War. At this point the Officer of marines breaks in and announces emotionally that Billy's motive was neither mutiny nor homicide.

Although Captain Vere agrees that in a civil trial there are many circumstances in the case which might excuse or lessen the foretopman's guilt and is certain that on the Day of Judgment, Billy will be acquitted, he reports that right here and now they can do nothing but "proceed under the law of the Mutiny Act" which deals specifically with crimes during time of war. All here are forced to fight for the King, he continues, some against their will, some even perhaps against their consciences. They are at war and all must stand united against one common enemy, the French Directory. "Budd's intent or non-intent is nothing to the purpose."

Respectful of their anxieties, he goes on to say that it is unbecoming to prolong what should be a quick decision, for the enemy may be sighted momentarily. Either condemn him or let him go. When the Lieutenant asks if they may convict Billy and yet soften the penalty, Captain Vere asks him to consider the consequences of such a merciful step. Surely the crew knows the traditions of the navy. Even if the situation could be explained to them, would they have the intelligence to understand the officers' reason for acting as they did? No, all they would see would be a "homicide committed in a flagrant act of mutiny." What would happen if they then learned that no penalty is to fall on Billy's head, but take the mercy shown to Billy for cowardice and all discipline would be destroyed. There might even be an outbreak if the men believed the officers were afraid of offending them by carrying out the demands of martial law in this instance. No, the crimes must be swiftly punished "lest it should provoke new troubles."

He leaves the three officers to their decision. Though disagreeing with many of the Captain's points, they felt disinclined to go against one superior in mind and rank. What really convinced them of course was his final warning of potential mutiny and trouble which might arise from too lenient treatment of a subordinate who kills his superior.

Their need to resolve the matter recalls an execution of three mutinous sailors aboard the U.S. brig-of-war Somers in 1842. Though not far from shore and in time of peace, they were punished and a subsequent court of inquiry vindicated the Commander's decision. The situation is different on the Indomitable but the sense of urgency was the same.

Although historians may criticize the action years afterward, a present emergency demands immediate action. Thus, Billy was formally convicted and sentenced to be hanged at the yard-arm in the early morning watch. If it were not nighttime, the sentence could have been carried out at once, for the punishment of a drum-head court decree in time of war is always carried out without appeal and without delay after a conviction.

Comment

Captain Vere's strange behavior during the trial reveals to us that there has been a miscarriage of justice. And after questioning

Billy, Captain Vere paces the cabin floor, then climbs "the slant deck in the ship's lee roll; thus without knowing it, he symbolizes by his actions a mind resolute to surmount difficulties even if against primitive instincts strong as the wind and the sea."

When Captain Vere is introduced, his chief characteristic is his brilliant intellect, by means of which he can now justify the overprudence that leads to injustice. In the trial itself he does not act on reason but chiefly on the emotion of fear. The reader recalls Melville's earlier discussion of Lord Nelson's successful way with a mutinous crew (Chapter 5) and, by contrast, how sordid and mean is Captain Vere's confrontation with major problems. Captain Vere's rationalizations of a virtuous expediency are in fact a perversion of justice.

By shifting responsibility for his decision to the King, Captain Vere denies that he can act as a free agent with a private conscience. The problem of whether Man possesses free will or is, instead, acted upon by Fate, is a major **theme** of Melville's and appears as a major theme in *Moby Dick*. If, like Captain Vere, one accepts the present state of the world, one must also accept the universal articles of war on which civilizations rest. Crime may be punished, but beauty and innocence will suffer far more in the process.

Billy as a Christ symbol is again called to mind. Both Billy and Christ were guiltless of the charge of treason brought against them, yet the charge was necessary for their official condemnation and execution, even though all judges at each of the trials knew all the charges to be false.

The naval enemy is referred to as "the regicidal French Directory," because King Louis XVI had been beheaded during the Revolution. The Directory was the executive council of the

French First Republic (1795-1799). It is this Directory which the British fleet is now fighting.

CHAPTER TWENTY-THREE

Captain Vere himself related the court's decision to Billy. What occurred at this interview in the small compartment which served as the foretopman's cell was not known. However, in view of the unusual character of each some guesses may be made.

It is most likely that the Captain held nothing back in his conference and related his role in the trial as well as his motives. Billy probably received the information in the same honest and sincere spirit in which it was offered. He must have been pleased that the Captain himself had made him his personal confidant and had spoken to him as one not afraid to die. A strong paternal feeling such as Abraham felt when he was about to sacrifice the young Isaac probably arose in the Captain's heart. Beyond these conjectures, it is impossible to state the exact context of the interview.

The senior Lieutenant, the first person to meet Captain Vere after leaving Billy's compartment, is startled by the expression of agony in the man's face, and he senses that Captain Vere is suffering far more intensely than the doomed foretopman.

Comment

To test Abraham's loyalty God ordered him to sacrifice his son Isaac to Him. Abraham built an altar, arranged wood on it, then bound his son to it. Just as the sorrowful father was about to slay his son with a knife, an angel's voice told him not to kill Isaac because the Lord was pleased with his unyielding obedience. (Genesis xxii: 1-14). Melville suggests that the relationship of Abraham to Isaac is similar to that of Captain Vere and Billy. While Isaac didn't die, still both "fathers" (Captain Vere "was old enough to have seen Billy's father") obeyed the law with blind obedience and with fear and trembling. Although neither made the law, each is forced to obey it, because each is subject to a power beyond himself.

Captain Vere may also be compared with Pontius Pilate. Like Pilate, he condemns a man whom he knows to be innocent and just to a shameful death. However, unlike Pilate, Captain Vere does not wash his hands of the trial, but assumes responsibility and takes the bitterness of the execution upon himself.

CHAPTER TWENTY-FOUR

Between the time Billy entered the Captain's cabin for the drumhead court trial and now when Captain Vere leaves his quarters "as one condemned to die," one and a half hours have elapsed. And, missing Billy, the crew began to speculate what he and the Master-at-arms were doing in the Captain's cabin. Rumor spread that both had entered it, but neither had emerged and suspense ran high.

When all hands were summoned on deck, the men were prepared for something out of the ordinary. The marine guard lined up on the quarter deck, and Captain Vere, surrounded by his officers, addressed the crew. In his official manner he used clear terms to describe the events in the cabin, Claggart's death, and Billy's trial and forthcoming execution. He carefully, however, avoided mention of the word "mutiny" as well as any preaching on the necessity of maintaining discipline, thinking that the "consequence of violating discipline should be made to speak for itself."

The crew, hearing all this, was struck dumb, but soon there began a confused and growing murmur which was immediately suppressed by the whistles of the boatswain. Almost immediately the Master-at-arms was given a funeral with all the honor belonging to his naval grade. For this service as well as for Billy's treatment the officers had to adhere to the proper rules, otherwise the ship's company would think something was amiss.

It is important in a military ship that the officers do not admit that they expect any trouble with the men. On the Indomitable, proceeding with caution, they kept a vigilant watch on the men. No one but the Chaplain was permitted to visit Billy.

CHAPTER TWENTY-FIVE

Billy had been transferred to one of the bays on the starboard side of the Indomitable's upper gun-deck. Surrounding the chained foretopman are guns and equipment for fighting. His white jumper and white duck trousers, though soiled, are the only shroud he will have. A flickering light reveals the cheek bone of the "Handsome Sailor" slightly defined under his rosetan skin, for "brief experiences devour our human tissue" in certain impassioned hearts.

Billy's agony, which resulted from "a generous young heart's virgin experience of the diabolical incarnate effective in some men," has lost all its tension and he is calm. Healed by Captain

Vere's private words, he lay in a trance, his face happy and gleaming as if reflecting some pleasant dream. The Captain enters, but noticing Billy's serene expression, he leaves, feeling that no consolation could bring to Billy greater peace than the one he now enjoys.

Very early in the morning he returns to Billy, who is awake and welcomes him. It becomes apparent that the Chaplain's task, "to bring Billy Budd to some Godly understanding that he must die," is unnecessary, for Billy is aware that he must die and is wholly without any irrational fear of it, a fear more common among the civilized than among those, such as Billy, who are not. At this moment Billy resembles those early blond English natives known as Angles, who were taken to Rome where they were described by Pope Gregory as Angels.

Without success the Chaplain tried to instill in Billy a fear of death as well as thoughts "of salvation and a Saviour." Billy, however, listened politely and regarded all that the man said as mariners always regard any discussion out of touch with their work-a-day world. The Chaplain decides not to press the lad, sensing that "innocence was even a better thing than religion wherewith to go to Judgment," and he leaves after kissing Billy on the cheek, an unheard of thing to do to a criminal sentenced to death. Although he is aware he can never convert Billy to his dogma, he does not fear for Billy's future.

Is it not strange that the Chaplain after meeting such an innocent youth (and a challenge to his own religious convictions as to the essential sinful nature of man) does nothing to prevent the doom "of such a martyr to martial discipline?" Of course, to do so would be futile and would violate the bounds of his function, for he is "the minister of the Prince of Peace serving in the host of the God of War-Mars."

Comment

It is significant that Billy's shroud should be white to symbolize his innocence. Melville reinforces his 'noble savage' **theme** with an extensive paragraph in this chapter. The "so-called barbarous" communities are superior to civilization, for it is the warm-hearted barbarian who stands closer to "unadulterated Nature," and not civilized man with his developed intellect and corrupted heart. Billy is like those barbarian ancestors who were paraded as trophies if the Roman triumph of Germanicust(famous Roman general and conqueror, 15 B.C. - 19 A.D.).

Melville continues his description of Billy's physical beauty, which is the outward glow of an inward spiritual beauty, by suggesting that had Pope Gregory I (540-604), who had referred to the English as angels, lived in a later time, the rosebud complexion of Billy's ancestral barbarians would have recalled to him the seraphs of the great fresco painted by Fra Angelico (Italian friar of the fifteenth century), "plucking apples in the gardens of the Hesperides" (in classical mythology the Hesperides were beautiful gardens where golden apples grew, guarded by a dragon).

Melville compares the Chaplain to a famous missionary of Captain Cook's time (a famous British explorer, 1728-1779), who had attempted to convert the South Sea Islanders. Although they politely listened to him, they would not accept what they heard. More than once in Melville's career he satirized the attempt of missionaries to convert a 'pagan' people. (cf. *Typee*).

Because the Chaplain, "the minister of Christ," receives his salary from Mars, the God of War, he is compared to that "musket of Blucher" (famous Prussian Field Marshal, 1742-1819, who had helped Wellington at Waterloo). "Why then is he there?" Melville queries, and answers critically, to lend "the sanction of the religion of the meek" to that military system which abolishes everything "but brute Force."

Billy, like little Pip in *Moby Dick*, is doomed through no fault other than innate innocence, and he too learns tragically that the ways of heaven are not the ways of this world. The harsh truth is that the good people in life are trusting. Perhaps Melville is here suggesting that we must not let evil remain unchallenged but fight it, since in Billy we have a demonstration of what happens when man is unaware of evil and does not resist it.

Although Billy is willing to die like Isaac and Christ, his death, though noble, remains unjust. If Captain Vere had the nobility and strength of Billy, he would not have allowed the foretopman to die. The lesson is, of course, that Billy learns to accept the obligatory harshness of the law, and that in the high impersonality of the law there is no distinction. As a result, it is dangerous both to the individual and to society.

CHAPTER TWENTY-SIX

At four o'clock in the morning the boatswain's whistles summoned all hands on deck to witness the punishment. And quickly all the men appeared, though none spoke a word. Captain Vere stood near the break of the poop-deck facing forward.

Since the hanging was to take place from the main-yard, Billy was brought there, accompanied by the Chaplain. It was noted at the time and commented upon later that the minister was genuinely interested in the foretopman, for although he gave a small sermon, his manner toward Billy displayed a much truer Gospel. As all watched expectantly, Billy at the moment just before he was about to hang, exclaimed without stumbling his last words, "God bless Captain Vere." Words so unexpected and which, expressed "in the clear melody of a singing-bird on the point of launching from the twig," moved the entire crew of the ship to consciously echo the sympathetic utterance. Billy was in their hearts, even as he was in their eyes. Captain Vere, either through the power of self-control or a momentary paralysis brought on by emotional shock, stood rigidly still.

At the moment of Billy's death, "it chanced that the vapory fleece hanging low in the East, was shot thru' with a soft glory as of the fleece of the Lamb of God seen in mystical vision," and to everyone's amazement, the body remained perfectly still. The only motion was caused by the motion of the ship.

Comment

Billy's cry of "God bless Captain Vere" (recalling Christ's utterance on the cross: "Father, forgive them; for they know not what they do." Luke 23:34) is a crowning **irony**. In addition, the description of Billy's death suggests the Ascension of Christ, for Melville, in the original manuscript, wrote 'Shekinah' and later substituted 'rose' ("took the full rose of the dawn.") In Jewish theology, Shekinah was the divine presence, or a radiance forming the visible manifestation of the divine presence. In the next chapter a reference to Billy's ascension' was later altered to Billy's "execution." These meaningful phrases reinforce the Christ-Billy Budd motif.

CHAPTER TWENTY-SEVEN

Some days after Billy's hanging, the Purser, a "ruddy rotund person more accurate as an accountant than profound as a philosopher," while eating with the Surgeon, asks the doctor if he thinks Billy's absolutely motionless death was due to will power. The Surgeon, a gloomy and at times sarcastic man, replies that in typical hangings all movement originating in the body after suspension causes death indicates "a mechanical spasm in the muscular system," and adds that the absence of the spasm in Billy's case can more be due to will power than to "horsepower." When asked whether muscular spasms occur without exception after hangings, and responding that they do, he is asked to explain their absence in the foretopman's case. To this seemingly unanswerable question, the Surgeon responds that the Purser seems to be involved with this incident whereas he himself is not. Although he cannot explain the absence of spasms, he resolutely refuses to accept the notion that there is not a valid scientific explanation for "the phenomenon that followed." And when the Purser seizes upon the word and suggests that they are in agreement that the absence of spasmodic movement was a "phenomenon," the Surgeon qualifies his statement, explaining that it was phenomenal "in the sense that it was an appearance," the cause of which is not understood.

The Purser however is not one to give up easily and asks the Surgeon if Billy's death was affected by the halter or "was it a species of euthanasia?" But the Surgeon, annoyed at the mention of the last word which he classifies with will power as unscientific, continues, "euthanasia is at once imaginative and **metaphysical**, - in short, Greek." Anxious to leave, he excuses himself by referring to a case which needs his medical assistance and departs.

Comment

In this chapter Melville mockingly describes the Surgeon's complete lack of faith in the seemingly spiritual aura which surrounds Billy's death, and is thus attacking his century's materialism and skepticism.

In death by hanging, involuntary spasms take place, but did not in Billy's. The Surgeon, expressing the scientific attitude, rejects what he cannot touch or explain (will power), while defining his terms by rote. His science is built on absolute laws of cause and effect which admit of no peculiarities; the absence of the spasm is related to perfectly natural but unknown laws according to the Surgeon's interpretation.

"Euthanasia" is a Greek word meaning easy, peaceful death. This, too, the Surgeon rejects because it conflicts with his scientific law. Among the Greeks this term had another meaning, the willful sacrifice of one's self for one's country. We can infer from the statements that he does not believe in free will, since he believes that all behavior can be explained in scientific terms. Such terms would, of course, exclude all consideration of the divine or supernatural.

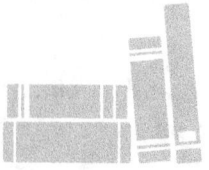

BILLY BUDD

TEXTUAL ANALYSIS

CHAPTERS 28–31

CHAPTER TWENTY-EIGHT

The silence at the moment of Billy's execution continues for a few moments afterwards, followed by a gradual murmuring sound arising among the crew. Their ill-humored sounds seem to imply that they wish to call back their repetition of Billy's blessing on Captain Vere. But before the murmur has a chance to grow louder, the Boatswain and his mates are ordered to blow their whistles which restore the men to discipline. Half depart and the remainder perform their duties.

Following a drum-head trial, everything is promptly and quickly carried out. Billy's hammock has been prepared to serve as his coffin, and a second call for all men brings everyone on the deck for his burial. At the body slides into the sea from the tilted plank, a second strange human murmur is heard blending with the sounds of a sea fowl who neared the burial site.

The drum beat to quarters is quickly sounded although it was an hour ahead of its usual time, and the martial discipline instilled in the men for so long makes them obey the call swiftly. The crowds dissolve and each man stands erect at his post while the First Officer formally receives the successive reports of the lieutenants, then delivers the total report to the Commander. This action pleases Captain Vere who had earlier noticed evidence of the necessity for breaking the almost rebellious mood of his men. "With mankind," he would say, "forms, measured forms are everything." The band plays a sacred hymn and the Chaplain performs the regular morning service. The drums then beat a retreat and the men disperse in their usual orderly manner. "The fleece of low-hanging vapor had vanished, licked up by the sun, that late had so glorified it."

Comment

Where pure 'head' (represented by the Surgeon) sees natural but unknown causes in everything, pure 'heart' (the sailors recognize supernatural forces at work) sees a religious meaning in the assembly of sea fowl over Billy's grave.

Orpheus in Greek mythology was a Thracian prince who was given the gift of music. So beautifully did he play his lyre that his music tamed wild beasts. Captain Vere uses Orpheus as a symbol to express his view that the world was ruled by "forms" or laws.

CHAPTER TWENTY-NINE

In this chapter Melville ties up the loose strands of his story. Under the Directory of France, the battleship St. Louis was renamed the Atheiste, a very apt name for a warship. The Atheiste encounters the Indomitable on its return trip to the English fleet, and in the ensuing battle, Captain Vere, attempting to place his ship alongside the other to capture it, is seriously wounded by a musket ball. He drops to the deck and is carried below. The senior Lieutenant takes command and successfully captures the enemy ship and manages to get to Gibraltar where the wounded, including Captain Vere, are put ashore. The Captain lingers on for some days, then dies, missing the later victories of Admiral Nelson at Trafalgar (1805), where he put an end to the French naval wars. Not long before his death, Captain Vere was heard to murmur under the influence of a soothing drug the words later related to the officer of marines on the Indomitable, "Billy Budd, Billy Budd."

Comment

Fighting the Atheiste, Captain Vere gave his life in defense of civilized existence in opposition to what were to him the destructive doctrines of the French Revolution. Thus the triumph of the Indomitable over the Atheiste seems the victory of order over chaos.

It is interesting to note that Pontius Pilate was haunted by the memory of Jesus Christ during his last years as praetor of Hispania Tarraconensis, not far from Gibraltar where Captain Vere murmurs Billy Budd's name as he lies dying.

CHAPTER THIRTY

Several weeks after the execution there appeared an account of the affair in an authorized naval chronicle. Although written in good faith, the author mixed rumor with fact, and, as a result, falsified the true events. According to this report the honest Master-at-arms discovered a mutinous plot led by one William Budd. In the process of arraigning the man before the Captain he was "vindictively stabbed to the heart by the suddenly drawn sheath-knife of Budd." The deed and the weapon used suggest that the assassin was mustered into service under an English name and was no real Englishman but one of those aliens which were admitted in large numbers in those difficult times. The enormity of the crime "and the extreme depravity of the criminal" were heightened in view of the "respectable and discreet" character of the petty officer upon whom "the efficiency of His Majesty's navy so largely depends." Although Claggart's function was a most responsible but a thankless task, he was faithful to it "because of his strong patriotic impulse." His character singly refuted Samuel Johnson's perverse remark that "patriotism is the last refuge of a scoundrel."

The criminal paid the full penalty and received his punishment promptly as was fitting. "Nothing amiss is now apprehended aboard the H.M.S. Indomitable."

This account appearing in an old, now forgotten publication was all that hitherto stood in human record "to attest what manner of men respectively were John Claggart and Billy Budd."

CHAPTER THIRTY-ONE

In navies everything is remarkable for a time. Any object associated with some unusual event becomes a monument. The spar from which Billy was suspended was kept track of over the years by the sailors, and when it was finally reduced to a dockyard boom, chips of it were prized as if they were bits from the Cross of Christ. Ignorant though the men were of the unknown causes of the tragedy and suspecting that the penalty "was somehow unavoidably inflicted from the naval point of view," they still felt instinctively that Billy was incapable of mutiny or willful murder. They recalled his youthful face, always bright and never expressing any internal ugliness of soul. The fact that he was gone, "in a measure mysteriously gone," added to his fame, and eventually an unskilled sailor turned his limited poetic talents to the subject of Billy and the **ballad** which he wrote was finally printed in Portsmouth.

The **ballad**, "Billy in the Darbies" (manacles or irons), ends the narrative. Billy, innocence personified, is not afraid but alone and sad since he is to hang the next day like a "pendant pearl from the yard-arm-end." He pictures going to his death on an empty stomach, being given a bite to eat and drink, the execution scene, and his burial when "they'll lash me in hammock, drop me deep." Longing for companionship and affection and wistfully recalling his friends, he contemplates his fate with sadness and resignation, "Fathoms down, fathoms down, now I'll dream fast asleep." The poem concludes, "I am sleepy, and the oozy weeds about me twist" - he already sees himself at the bottom of the ocean.

Comment

Captain Vere's whole argument was irrational and his final appeal was to brute force. The sailors instinctively perceived Billy's innocence. Theirs was the conflict between reason and instinct, the order of logic and the rebellion of emotion. They obscurely felt that Billy was unjustly and unnecessarily sacrificed and these views enter into the spirit of the poem.

The trite phrasing, such as "O, 'tis me, not the sentence they'll suspend" suggests perhaps that even the form of poetry cannot capture the essential truth of Billy Budd.

The poem represents Melville's final expression of faith in mankind, a faith in the ability of the common man to see beyond the distortions of truth, however disguised; a faith that the essential dignity, beauty, and heroism of man will always be recognized and celebrated in artistic form, however unpolished.

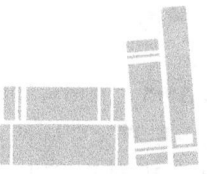

BILLY BUDD

CHARACTER ANALYSES

Billy Budd

A handsome, carefree, innocent foretopman aboard H.M.S. Indomitable. Recently impressed into the King's service from the merchantman, Rights of Man, where he had been the favorite of the crew and Captain Graveling's "Jewel," twenty-one year old Billy is a superb specimen of Anglo-Saxon manhood, tanned, healthy, and freehearted. He is, we are told, as innocent of evil as Adam before the fall, and is compared to Hercules, Apollo, and Alexander the Great. Billy is, however, cursed with a single blemish, a fatal flaw. When under the stress of strong emotion, "he has a tendency to stutter and sometimes even worse" (he cannot speak at all).

John Claggart

The Master-at-arms aboard the Indomitable, charged with maintaining order among the men of the lower gundeck. About thirty-five, he is spare and tall with shapely hands unaccustomed to toil. Because of a slight accent which marks him as other than English, and manners which mark him as a man of some education, it is rumored that prior to his enlistment in the navy he had been involved in some shady practices, rumors which account for his holding a position obviously beneath him. He had achieved his present rank rapidly after entering the have through "constitutional sobriety, ingratiating deference to his superiors," and a genius for securing information. He now maintains discipline among his subordinates with the help of his corporals through harassment and deception. Although he appears perfectly normal, he is actually a madman, depraved "according to nature." Careful in his dress, with a protuberant forehead and a pallid complexion, he appears to all a calm, self-controlled man. He is, however, the embodiment of all evil, capable of coolly directing his evil talents against any object of his hatred.

Captain Edward Fairfax "Starry" Vere

A bachelor of about forty, he is a distinguished captain in the Royal Navy. Regarded generally as reliable, honest, and capable by all who know him, he is characterized by a somewhat bookish manner of speech, a habit acquired through extensive reading. Before each voyage he restocks his small, but excellent library with books on common sense philosophy, history, and biography. And like the authors he reads, Captain Vere is a conservative who objects to the revolutionary tendencies of the age because he cannot believe that rebellion and change can bring about permanent or effective institutions for the benefit of mankind. Like the English poet Alexander Pope, Captain Vere is a firm adherent of the philosophy which argues that "whatever is, is right." Although he is a stern disciplinarian, he is regarded with affection by those who serve under him, and is capable of inspiring loyalty in his crews. He is, however, generally called "Starry" Vere because of his disconcerting habit of gazing blankly at the sea. He lacks the ability to communicate with his subordinates in the customary good-humored manner of nautical men.

Dansker

An old battle-scarred sailor well-known among his navy shipmates because he had served with distinction under Admiral Nelson aboard the Agamemnon. Now too old to perform the normal duties of a seaman, he is assigned to watch duty near the main mast where, like an ancient wise man, he watches all that goes on about him. Although Dansker is eccentric and does not make friends easily among the younger sailors, he befriends Billy, upon whom he bestows the nickname of "Baby Budd," because Billy never passes him without a duly respectful greeting. Although he warns Billy of Claggart's hatred, he is unable to express his warning in terms which Billy is able to understand. Long experience as a subordinate had taught him to be wary of his superiors.

Squeak

A grizzled and sharp-eyed corporal of the lower gundeck, nicknamed Squeak by the crew because of his ratlike characteristics. As the immediate subordinate of Claggart, it is Squeak who carries out Claggart's petty harassment of Billy.

Lieutenant Ratcliffe

The young officer of the Indomitable who impresses Billy into naval service. A burly, bluff officer, he is the embodiment of that class of experienced and hardened seamen whose good humor enables them to enjoy life.

Captain Graveling

Captain of the Rights of Man, the merchant ship from which Billy is impressed. A kindly, efficient officer, he deeply regrets the loss of Billy whom he refers to as his "Jewel," his "peacemaker."

The Officers Of The Court-Martial - The First Lieutenant, The Captain Of Marines, And The Sailing Master

Although they are portrayed as capable, sympathetic men, they remain the faceless, nameless representatives of blind and unemotional justice.

The Surgeon

He is the embodiment of all those who follow the dictates of reason (science) alone. He explains Billy's quiet death as due to natural though unexplained causes.

The Chaplain

"A discreet man with the good sense of a good heart." As God's representative aboard a warship, he represents Melville's idea that good and evil exist side by side in the world.

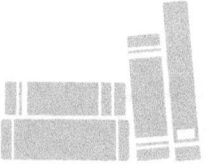

BILLY BUDD

CRITICAL COMMENTARY

Billy Budd, written in the last years of Melville's life, though ostensibly a simple tale of injustice, is actually a multi-leveled exploration of good and evil in the universe, and in many ways it represents a return by Melville to the irresistible **theme** of *Moby Dick*. That there is a difference, however, in the tone and method of *Billy Budd* from his earlier work cannot be doubted, and it is this difference as well as its own depth which has challenged innumerable able critics to attempt at least a partial illumination of it.

To many critics *Billy Budd* represents a working out of the eternal conflict between good and evil in orthodox Christian terms. And certainly the characters of the novel as well as the innumerable Biblical **allusions** lend much credence to this interpretation. Moreover, if the interpretation is even partially correct, it represents a reconciliation by Melville to the notion that good and evil may coexist in the universe, and a turning away by him from the rebellious attitudes of *Pierre* and *Moby Dick*. Thus, *Billy Budd*, according to Lewis Mumford, is the story of the world, the "spirit and the devil," and its message is that "good and evil exist in the nature of things, each itself, each doomed to war with the other." Evil then has a place as well as good. This is "the fundamental ambiguity of life." In general it is this view of *Billy Budd* which is accepted and promulgated by such critics as F. O. Matthiessen and R. W. B. Lewis.

Although other critics willingly admit Melville's use of religious symbolism in the working out of his tale, they insist that *Billy Budd* is "more political than theological or mythic." Most notable among these is Richard Chase, who argues that "society cannot be based on the contrary absolutes of evil and good represented by Billy Budd and his traducer Claggart." And this interpretation appears to have some validity. Surely Claggart and Billy are characters who represent the philosophic extremes of Rousseau and Hobbes. Billy is then the "natural man" free of the corruption caused by too long an association with the decadent institutions of organized society, and thus ideally represents Rousseau's concept of the "noble savage." Claggart, on the other hand, is Hobbes' man "naturally depraved" and evil, kept in check only by the restraints of custom and law. Of course, then, as a result of this interpretation, Captain Vere becomes the hero of the novel since he is the representative of a social order whose ideal is the middle way, a reconciliation of the apparent contradiction of good and evil. He is man neither good nor evil, but rather a man whose concept of "order, authority, and legality" makes him the "tragic hero" who, though conscious of good and evil, must act in obedience to the codes of an authority higher than himself. This interpretation, too, of course, represents a kind of reconciliation for the always rebellious Melville. For in this case it is the Veres of the world who are valid and not the Billys nor Claggarts who are doomed to destroy each other through eternal conflict.

Still other critics, including Leonard Caspar, disagree that *Billy Budd* represents Melville's "testament of acceptance."

Indeed, when Melville describes Claggart as an irrational being who hides behind a reasonable exterior, does not such a description apply equally to Captain Vere? Surely Captain Vere's sudden change of attitude toward Billy, and his decision at Billy's summary trial are not the products of natural justice. Is not Vere's decision "a perversion as serious as Claggart's?" Nor does Billy's stoic acceptance of the consequences of Captain Vere's decision necessarily imply an acceptance of the injustice of that decision. He says only, "I seem fated to die, right or wrong, I am ready." What then seems clear is that he does not accept the justice of the decision, but rather accepts his fate.

Another group of critics interpret *Billy Budd* as Greek tragedy, and this too appears a valid possibility since most of the elements of tragedy are present. We have a hero, blemished only by a single "fatal flaw" which is to bring about his downfall. The story takes place over a short span of time, in a single place, and presents but a single action. And in addition Claggart appears as the human representative of a malevolent fate whose sole function is the destruction of the hero. And Billy, like the tragic hero, is warned by the oracle or seer, Dansker, of his possible fate, and like the tragic hero he cannot understand the warning until it is too late.

The difficulty of interpreting *Billy Budd* must by now be clear, for *Billy Budd* presents Melville's view that life is a "colossal ambiguity, a series of paradoxes." Indeed, although most of the commentators on *Billy Budd* have helped to shed much light, the difficulty is that *Billy Budd* does not admit of a single or simple interpretation. For example, if we accept that Biblical interpretation which argues that *Billy Budd* is the retelling of the story of Christ, we are confronted with the difficulty of explaining Billy's "fatal flaw," his stuttering, and his lack of awareness of the evil which confronts him. Nor is

Billy's goodness explained as the result of any effort or desire upon his own part, but merely the result of having successfully avoided evil. And further, Captain Vere fails as a satisfactory "God." First he vacillates and then acts in a manner contrary to his own innermost desires. And finally Claggart fails in the role of Satan, for unlike the Satan of the Bible, he has neither stature nor sufficient motivation.

The same difficulties of interpretation are also encountered by those explanations of *Billy Budd* which account for the story as the embodiment of some political, social, or philosophic belief. Though surely Melville is critical of those laws and institutions represented by Captain Vere and the Articles of War, and the two worlds represented by the Rights of Man and the Atheiste, it is just as obvious that he is not entirely critical of them. Not only is Captain Vere treated sympathetically, but life aboard the Indomitable is not without its compensations. There, in spite of the hardships imposed by the severity of naval discipline, Billy, with the lone exception of Claggart, found the same understanding and good fellowship which he had enjoyed aboard the Rights of Man.

Nor do those interpretations of *Billy Budd* as tragedy provide an ultimate explanation. For although Billy possesses most of the necessary attributes of a tragic hero, he lacks the stature and the tragic sense of awareness which is the hallmark of tragedy. To be a tragic hero, one must feel greatly. Not only can Billy not understand the nature of evil, he lacks even the most rudimentary awareness of it. And finally, the tragedy which must eventually befall a tragic hero (at least in the classical sense) is to fall from high place or station in life.

Unfortunately these comments cannot do justice to the almost endless possibilities of interpretation to be found in *Billy

Budd. Though most interpretations must ultimately fall short of a total explanation of the meaning of *Billy Budd*, nearly all have provided a new way of looking at it. Probably the greatest testimony of the novel's value is to be found in the complex and ambiguous nature of its composition. Because it is so multi-faceted, each new light exposes a new surface to view. This and the elemental problem of good and evil which the novel explores, then, will undoubtedly continue to attract and transfix its readers for a long time to come.

BILLY BUDD

ESSAY QUESTIONS AND ANSWERS

Question: How does Melville create character in *Billy Budd*?

Answer: First, Melville in *Billy Budd* invariably introduces his characters through the medium of an introductory sketch after which they enter into the narrative. These descriptive sketches provide the necessary background for each character and prepare the reader for the part each is to play in the narrative. Second, the characters are further developed by means of words or phrases which are repeatedly used to describe them, or by means of characteristic phrases which they repeatedly utter. For example, Billy Budd is many times referred to as the "Handsome Sailor" or "Baby Budd"; Captain Vere by his nickname of "Starry" Vere; and Dansker, by his repetition of "Jemmy Legs is down on you." Third, the characters in *Billy Budd* are developed through repeated references to their appearance. The strangely sallow Claggart, the dreamy, aristocratic Captain Vere, and the scarred and wrinkled Dansker are all contrasted with the handsome, carefree Billy. So too is each description a reflection of the real character of each.

Question: How does Melville use literary, Biblical, historical, and mythological **allusion** to reinforce his story?

Answer: Through the repeated use of appropriate **allusion**, the characters in *Billy Budd* are intensified and the events of the plot foreshadowed. For example, Billy Budd is compared to Hercules, Apollo, and Alexander the Great as a means of underscoring his strength, handsomeness, and noble nature. And when he is compared to Caspar Hauser, a young man who had been murdered in Nuremburg in 1833, and to Adam before his fall from paradise, the evil that is to befall him is foreshadowed. In addition, the comparisons of Claggart to Shawnee, the renegade Indian chief, and Titus Oates, the plotter against Charles II, and finally to Ananias, who was struck dead for lying to God (Acts v: 1-5), reveal more clearly his evil and treacherous nature. Further, the comparison of Claggart and Billy to Chang and Eng, the famous Siamese twins of the mid-nineteenth century who were joined together in life and death, is a dark hint of the relationship between them. The **allusions** to Captain Vere which compare him to Admiral Nelson, Don John of Austria, and Andrea Doria emphasize his unusual ability and his inflexible nature. And so too, those **allusions** which compare Dansker to the seers and oracles of old intensify the mysterious nature of his character and foretell the fulfillment of his veiled warnings.

Question: What autobiographic material does Melville use in *Billy Budd*?

Answer: First, the novel is dedicated to Jack Chase who had served as a foretopman (like Billy Budd) with Melville during his hitch aboard the U.S. Frigate United States. Second, the story opens on the docks of Liverpool, England where Melville had stopped during his first voyage at sea aboard the St. Lawrence. Third, Melville draws extensively upon the experience of his adventurous years at sea for a knowledge of nautical terms and procedures to provide a realistic background, and upon his wide reading for a wealth of historical, literary, Biblical, and mythological allusion.

Question: What advantages are achieved by Melville's limiting the action of his story to only those events which occur aboard the Indomitable?

Answer: By limiting his story principally to those events which occur aboard the Indomitable, Melville is able to limit the action of his story and the number of characters involved. Among the benefits of such limitation are the fact that each character may be studied in considerable depth, and the significant interaction between the characters explored in all their ramifications. The severely limited world of *Billy Budd* is thus a microcosm of the larger world, and the events which occur in that little world are a kind of moral parable by which the larger world may be better understood. And, finally, since the action of the story is limited to a single significant event, the reader's attention is not distracted by innumerable trivialities, but is rather focused upon those questions concerning the mystery of life which the parables pose for him.

Question: How does Melville's method of characterization help him to develop his themes?

Answer: For the most part, Melville's characters in *Billy Budd* are "larger than life." Not only are they representative of individual men, but they are also representative of general classes of men. Billy is the symbol of all who are free and unfettered. Without family or connection, he lives the simple and honest life of a sailor, unsoiled by too long a contact with the corrupting influence of society. As Adam before the fall, he is what man might have been. As Billy is the representative of all that is good, Claggart is unregenerate, absolute evil; he is the serpent in Billy's Eden. And as such, he is not only Billy's tempter, but also Billy's destroyer. As Billy and Claggart are symbolic of the extremes of good and evil, Captain Vere is the symbol of intelligent, educated, and civilized man who is neither essentially good nor bad, but potentially either. He is blindly obedient to those unchanging and often unjust codes which are imposed upon men by an impersonal social order. When Billy, the agent of active good, accidentally kills Claggart, who is active evil, he is condemned by Captain Vere, who remains only the passive and unquestioning agent of a supposedly civilized society. Thus the **themes** of *Billy Budd* are neither simple nor completely identifiable, but at least the reader is provoked to thought about the nature of good and evil, and about man's capacity to achieve justice and order in a complex and confused world.

Question: How and why does Melville interrupt the main narrative of *Billy Budd*?

Answer: Melville frequently interrupts the main narrative of the story to supply his reader with necessary background material. Although most of the necessary background of the novel has been supplied in the preface, other essential information is supplied in places closer to those sections of the book where the material is more appropriate, and in almost every instance the interjected material contains a **foreshadowing** of events to come. For example, immediately following the introduction of Captain Vere, the long descriptive section on his background supplies us with the information that he is an extremely competent though conservative officer, and again reminds us that the mutinies at Spithead and Nore are events of the recent past, fresh in the minds of most commanders. We are thus prepared for Captain Vere's summary condemnation of Billy under the Articles of War.

So too are we prepared for Claggart's false accusation from that first extensive description of his naturally depraved character. In addition to supplying necessary information, these extended interruptions of the narrative also serve as a means of creating suspense in an otherwise simple and straightforward tale whose plot, like a Greek Tragedy, is almost entirely predictable.

Question: What are some of the major critical interpretations of *Billy Budd*, and what are some of the limitations of those interpretations?

Answer: Because of Melville's extensive use of **allusion**, Biblical, literary, and historical, there have been many attempts to interpret *Billy Budd* as at least a partial allegory by stressing one or another of his lines of **allusion** and playing down the others. For example, many critics view *Billy Budd* as evidence of Melville's return to orthodox Christianity, and certainly there is a wealth of Biblical **allusion** to justify such a possible interpretation. If we see Billy as Christ, Captain Vere as God the Father, and Claggart as Satan, *Billy Budd* becomes a retelling of the story of Christ. We must, however, always bear in mind that both the story and its characters are multi-allusioned rather than single, with the result that no single interpretation is ever likely to be fully satisfactory. Surely Billy is not Christ, for he is stained with an imperfection in speech, nor does he fully comprehend the implication of his death. Nor is Captain Vere a sufficiently grand figure to represent God, since his vacillations are all too human. And Claggart, although he represents absolute evil, is evil according "to nature" and not absolutely evil. If we view *Billy Budd* according to the many and varied philosophic and social interpretations, the same difficulties are apparent. For example, if Billy is Rousseau's Natural Man, "The Noble Savage," and Captain Vere is unnatural man because he has been corrupted by too long an association with civilization, we are at a loss to explain Claggart, "a depravity according to nature" - and a contradiction of Rousseau's concept of Natural Goodness.

What then must ultimately become obvious for the serious reader is that *Billy Budd* is not a simple novel. Because of its vast wealth of **allusions** and richness of suggestion, it may admit of multiple interpretations, all of which have varying degrees of validity. And it is this very multi-faceted nature of the novel which accounts for its ability to intrigue critic and reader alike. Like all great literature, its depth makes it possible for each to uncover some new treasure with each reading.

BILLY BUDD

GLOSSARY OF NAUTICAL TERMS

....

Aft - toward or near the stern-as opposed to fore of bow of a ship.

Allotted To The Pipe - that part of the lower gundeck where smoking was allowed.

Beam - measurement across a ship as opposed to its length.

Bells - a nautical means of telling time. The day is divided into six watches of four hours each and eight bells are rung at four, eight, and twelve o'clock. At twelve-thirty one bell, at one o'clock two bells, and so on until eight bells, and the procedure is repeated over again.

Bridle - a loop of rope used to furl or restrain a ship's sail when not in use.

Brig - a two-masted, square-rigged vessel. (The Indomitable is probably a frigate like the United States on which Melville had served during his navy service, since it is described as a moderate sized warship, carrying three masts, fore, main, and mizzen, each of which carries a number of sails.)

Bulwark - the raised side of a ship above the upper deck.

Darbies - manacles or irons.

Dead Eye - a round flat block of wood with three holes in it for the lanyard.

Dog Watch - one of the two two-hour watches between four and eight P.M.

Earing - a small rope for the attaching of the upper corner of a sail to a yard or gaff.

Fiddlehead - a carved decoration on a ship's bow like the scroll of a violin's head.

Forecastle - the upper deck of a ship in front of the foremast; the forepart of a ship where the sailor's quarters are located.

Hardtack - a hard biscuit baked in round cakes without salt used by sailors on long voyages when other types of stores might spoil.

Jonah's Toss - the putting overboard of someone or something considered unlucky.

Lanyard - a short rope or cord used on ships to fasten things.

Lee - the sheltered side of ship as opposed to windward.

Midshipman - a petty officer in the British Navy; in the United States Navy, a naval cadet about to become an ensign.

Poop Deck - a deck above the main deck aft of the mizzenmast (stern).

Port - the left side of a ship looking forward from the stern toward the bow.

Post Captain - a captain of a British warship of three years standing, now simply captain.

Purser - a ship's officer in charge of accounts.

Quarter Deck - a part of the after section of the upper deck of a vessel (on sailing ships usually some part of the poop deck) reserved for some special purposes or ceremonies.

Rattan - a small cane or switch made of wickerwork often carried by petty officers as a sign of authority.

Spar - any pole, mast, yard, boom, or gaff which supports or extends sails on a ship.

Star-Deck - the upper deck running the full length of a ship.

Starboard - the right side of a ship looking forward from the stern toward the bow.

Taffrail - a rail around a ship's stern.

Tar - an old name for sailors, since on early sailing ships they tarred the rope rigging to preserve it from the elements.

Yardarm - either end of a yard or cross-spar supporting a square sail.

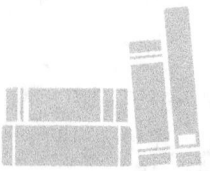

HERMAN MELVILLE

BIBLIOGRAPHY AND GUIDE TO RESEARCH

Among the many excellent books and articles on Herman Melville, the two best introductory works are James C. Miller's *A Reader's Guide to Herman Melville* (1962 Paperback), and Floyd Stovall's *Eight American Authors*. Each contains the complete standard text of *Billy Budd*. The following is a highly selective list of the most important criticism arranged by author within key research topics, with the exception of the biographies which are arranged chronologically.

BIOGRAPHIC STUDIES (ARRANGED CHRONOLOGICALLY)

Mumford, Lewis. *Herman Melville*. New York: Harcourt Brace and Company, 1929. A good earlier study of Melville which develops the notion of his imaginative genius.

Arvin, Newton. *Herman Melville: A Critical Biography*. New York: The Viking Press Inc., 1957. Available in paperback by Compass Books. Most readable of all, if not the most factual biography.

Howard, Leon. *Herman Melville: A Biography*. Berkeley: University of California Press, 1952. Probably the most trustworthy regarding facts.

Leda, Jay (Ed.). *The Melville Log* (1951). A compendium of data about Melville, arranged chronologically in two volumes.

HERMAN MELVILLE AND HIS SOURCES

Questions to consider: What were Melville's sources for *Billy Budd*? How much of *Billy Budd* is autobiographical? How did Melville adapt his sources to his purpose?

Anderson, Charles R. "The Genesis of *Billy Budd*," *American Literature* xxi (1940-1941), pp. 328-346.

Braswell, William. "Melville's *Billy Budd* as 'An Inside Narrative'," *American Literature* xxix (May, 1957), pp. 133-146.

Freeman, F. Barron. "Introduction," *Herman Melville's Billy Budd*. Cambridge: Harvard University Press, 1948. pp. 1-126. Excellent analysis of varied aspects of *Billy Budd*, including background, sources, style, and criticism.

Pearson, Norman H. "*Billy Budd*: The King's Yarn," *American Quarterly* III (Summer, 1951), pp. 91-114. A good discussion of the literary **allusions** in *Billy Budd*.

Stafford, William. *Melville's Billy Budd and the Critics*. San Francisco: University of California Press, 1961. A valuable collection of material from various sources on many aspects of Melville and *Billy Budd*.

RELIGIOUS AND ETHICAL BACKGROUND

Questions to consider: What does *Billy Budd* reveal about Melville's religious or ethical beliefs? Does *Billy Budd* represent for Melville a change of attitude from his earlier works? How did Melville employ religious symbolism to reinforce the meaning of his work?

Braswell, William. *Melville's Religious Thought*. Durham: Duke University Press, 1943. Still the most complete study of this aspect of Melville.

Mason, Ronald. *The Spirit above the Dust, A Study of Herman Melville*. London: John Lehmann, Ltd., 1951. pp. 245-260.

Sedgwick, W. E. *Herman Melville: The Tragedy of the Mind*. Cambridge: Harvard University Press, 1944. pp. 231-249. A discussion of the development of Melville's "inner vision," and *Billy Budd* as acceptance in contrast to *Typee, Redburn*, and *Pierre*.

Thompson, Lawrence. "Divine Depravity," *Melville's Quarrel with God*. Princeton: Princeton University Press, 1952. An extensive study of the irony of *Billy Budd*, and of Melville's beliefs with regard to God.

Tindall, William York. "The Ceremony of Innocence," in R. M. McIver ed., *Great Moral Dilemmas in Literature, Past and Present*. New York: Harper and Brothers, 1956. pp. 73-81.

Watson, E. L. G. "Melville's Testament of Acceptance," *New England Quarterly* vi (1932), pp. 319-327.

Walters, R. E. "Melville's Metaphysics of Evil," *University of Toronto Quarterly* ix (1940), pp. 170-182.

Weaver, Raymond M. *Herman Melville: Mariner and Mystic*. New York: George H. Doran Co., 1921. Reissued as a Pageant Book, New York, 1960.

Wright, Nathalia. *Melville's Use of the Bible.* Durham: Duke University Press, 1949, pp. 126-136. A valuable source book for those interested in Melville's Biblical sources of language, **theme**, character and image.

SOCIAL, POLITICAL AND CULTURAL BACKGROUND

Questions to be considered. What are the social and political implications of *Billy Budd*? How do Melville's social and political beliefs compare with those of his contemporaries? Is *Billy Budd* a novel out of place in the mainstream of American literature? - When it was written? Today?

Chase, Richard. *Herman Melville: A Critical Study.* New York: MacMillan, 1949. Stresses the mythic and psychological aspects of Melville, both as an artist and in relation to cultural problems.

Chase, Richard. "A Note on *Billy Budd,*" *The American Novel and its Tradition.* New York: Doubleday Anchor Books, 1957, pp. 113-115. Contains a political interpretation of *Billy Budd.*

Matthiessen, F. O. "Billy Budd, Foretopman," *American Renaissance.* New York: Oxford University Press, 1941, pp. 500-514.

Schneider, Herbert W. *A History of American Philosophy.* Columbia University Press, 1946.

GENERAL CRITICISM AND FURTHER BIBLIOGRAPHIC AND DISCUSSION SOURCES

Gettman, Royal A., and Bruce Harkness. "Billy Budd Foretopman," *Teacher's Manual for a Book of Stories.* New York: Rinehart & Co., Inc., 1955, pp. 71–74. Presents possible discussion material for classroom use.

Schiffman, Joseph. "Melville's Final Stage, **Irony**: A Reexamination of *Billy Budd* Criticism," *American Literature* xxii (May, 1950), pp. 128-136.

Stallman, R. W., and R. E. Watters. *The Creative Reader*. New York: The Ronald Press Co., 1954, pp. 334-338. A general reader which provides notes and questions for general discussion.

For those interested in more recent articles on *Billy Budd*, see the annual bibliographies (May issues) of *P.M.L.A.* (*Publication of the Modern Language Association*), the quarterly issues of *American Literature*, and the monthly issues of *Abstracts of English Studies*.

www.ingramcontent.com/pod-product-compliance
Lightning Source LLC
LaVergne TN
LVHW011728060526
838200LV00051B/3072